BETWEEN CHRIST AND SATAN

by
Kurt E. Koch, Th.D.

KREGEL PUBLICATIONS
Grand Rapids, Michigan 49501

 Translated from the German and published by the Evangelizations Publishers, West Germany, 1962. Published in the United States of America by Kregel Publications, a division of Kregel, Inc., P.O. 2607, Grand Rapids, Michigan 49501

Library of Congress Catalog Card No. 79-160690

ISBN 0-8254-3003-8

Printed in the United States of America

Contents

Foreword

To the uninstructed in the things of God the findings and facts presented in this volume may seem fanciful and farfetched. There are some who are totally unacquainted with the Saviour, the Lord Jesus Christ, and the transforming power of His gospel so that they do not know the reality nor even the possibility of the transfer of citizenship from the kingdom of Satan to the kingdom of God. There are many who know the Saviour as their own but are uninstructed in the Word of God so as to be strangers to the reality of spiritual warfare. Such know the power of the gospel to save from sin but not the authority of the name of the Lord Jesus Christ against Satan and his hosts.

There are many Christians, born again of the Spirit of God, who are unfamiliar with spiritual realities, either good or evil. They know about the Holy Spirit from the Scriptures and can repeat the Apostels' Creed in all honesty, saying, "I believe in the Holy Ghost." But the Holy Spirit is not a living, dynamic Personality to them, nor are demonic personalities a reality because such believers lack appreciation and discernment of things spiritual. They are like a person who hears music, vocal or instrumental, but have no understanding nor appreciation for it because of their insensitivity to music whether in harmony or discord. Such are the many who have no discernment of things spiritual.

There are some, however, to whom the triune God, Father, Son, and Holy Spirit are very real personalities. In particular they are acquainted with the indwelling of the Holy Spirit in the life of a believer in Christ, and they know the dreadful reality of spiritual warfare in the heavenlies and on earth from the beginning of the Scriptures to the end thereof, from the entrance of Satan into the Garden of Eden to his being cast into the Lake of Fire.

Demonic activity is not uniform the world over nor in historical experience. It appears that there was a great increase in demonic activity preceding and during the life of the Lord Jesus here on earth. There does appear to be a present increase because of an awareness on the part of the powers of darkness that their time is short and that the second coming of Christ is at hand. It is therefore particularly imperative for Christians to be informed in spiritual warfare.

Over the years I have met a few Christians who are so instructed. Usually they have been missionaries from the dark places of the earth. Some are pastors and laymen. Among the most informed and experienced that I have met is Dr. Kurt Koch, a Lutheran minister in Germany. This volume is one of many he has written to present his findings and facts regarding demonic activity and the effort for presenting a scriptural understanding therein. These facts are neither fancy nor the product of fanaticism. The Christian is to go forth into spiritual warfare fully armed as described in Ephesians 6, with faith in the all conquering name of the Lord Jesus Christ and without fear.

V. Raymond Edman
Chancellor
Wheaton College
Wheaton, Illinois

Preface

The well-known writer C. S. Lewis wrote in the preface to his book 'The Screwtape Letters':

"There are two equal and opposite errors into which our race can fall about the devils. One is to disbelieve in their existence. The other is to believe, and to feel an excessive and unhealthy interest in them."

On one side we have the rationalists of every shade and colouring and on the other side we have the magicians. Both of these groups of people will be upset by this book, and one might ask: have they reason to be? Whether they have or not, Christian ministers and counsellors are justified in being distressed when they meet the devastating effects of materialism and magic in their counselling sessions. It is thus our duty to publish the following information, and two reasons compel us to do so.

First of all we must proclaim the victory that Jesus Christ has won over the powers of darkness. People oppressed and subjected by occultism will never find true deliverance through medicine, psychology or psychiatry; it is only to be found in Jesus Christ. It is for us to show them the way to the Great Deliverer.

Secondly, people must be warned of the dangers of spiritism, magic and occultism. There are terrible consequences involved if we trespass into these areas, and God Himself has forbidden us to touch these things.

We will be drawing heavily upon examples brought to light in private counselling sessions, but in each case we have the express permission of those involved to publish the information.

The Author

Chapter One

Fortune-Telling

For thousands of years fortune-telling has been a bastard of heathenism, born out of fear, curiosity and superstition. Today fortune-telling is a many-sided problem involving folklore, psychology and theology. The following chapters had their origin in the counselling work of an evangelical minister and theologian. Such a ministry is a continual source of new material in this area. My file of occult cases has already grown to over 20,000 in number. In this present book we shall be avoiding scientific dissertations. Such an approach can be found in my book 'Christian Counselling and Occultism', but here we will be dealing mainly with first-hand examples, to enable the reader to form his own opinion. The seal of confession will not be violated since permission has been granted for the publishing of the instances found in this book. In this first chapter the following aspects of fortune-telling will be discussed: astrology, card-laying, palmistry, divination by rod and by pendulum, mirror mantic, psychometry; and finally we will consider the position taken by the Bible and the way to liberation from occult subjection.

(I) Astrology

Ex. 1. A woman appeared at a police station and stated that she had just shot and killed her son. An astrologer had told her in a written horoscope that her son would never regain his full mental health. Wanting to save the boy from this terrible future, she had killed him. The woman was arrested and finally sentenced after a long trial. The astrologer himself went free.

This day-to-day experience shows the suggestive powers and effects that horoscopes have. But before we enter this problematic field, first a brief historical introduction.

One understands by astrology the prediction of human character and destiny from the stars and their constellations. It is the most widely spread superstition of our time. The Research Institute of Public Opinion at Lake Constance established through a questionnaire that about 63 % of the German people had occupied themselves with astrology at one time or another. Very few of them know about the so-called scientific form of astrology, and most of them only subscribe to the solstitial point horoscope.

In the ancient world astronomy (the exploration of the stars) and astrology (the interpretation of the constellations of the stars) were a single science. In the ancient Babylonian Empire it was the science of the priests. Originally horoscopes were cast only for kings. Since astrology can also be traced back to ancient Mexican culture, it is thought to be a common human phenomenon and archetype. The Greeks and the Romans took over astrology from the Babylonians. Of course at that time there were already rational thinkers who ridiculed astrology. The poet Ennius declared, "Horoscopes cost one drachme, and are one drachme too expensive." The Church father Augustine called astrology the most stupid delusion of mankind!

During the Middle Ages, Europe was gripped by astrology. The Emperor Frederick II (1194–1250) was especially influenced by it. Professorial chairs for astrology were established. The reformer Philip Melanchthon even held one. Luther, however, called it 'a shabby art'. The story is told of how at that time the astrologer Stoeffler made a complete fool of himself. He predicted a diluvian flood for February 1524. The population was terrified. Nobody wanted to work. The fields were not tilled. The rich either had ships built for themselves or they retreated for safety into the mountains. Even the Elector of Brandenburg made preparations to escape the flood.

The great astronomer Kepler was also not free from the contamination of astrology. A well-known example of this is his prediction that Wallenstein would die a peaceful death in his 70th year. But he was killed in his 50th year. Yet Kepler only engaged in astrology out of economic necessity. He wrote, "Astrology is to me an unbearable but necessary slavery. To keep my yearly income, my title, and my living quarters, I have to comply with ignorant curiosity. Astronomy is the wise mother, and astrology the foolish daughter who gives herself to anyone who pays her, so that she can support her wise mother."

Since the age of rationalism (1750), however, astrology has declined in its influence. Astronomy and astrology finally parted company. But two world wars have made it flare up again. In 1930 horoscopes were already being cast for Hitler but they were very contradictory. After 1933 they said his influence should have declined. The 'truth' of these horoscopes we have certainly experienced. They contained a miscalculation of about twelve years, and what a disastrous twelve years they were! The horoscope of Rudolf Hess prophesied that he was destined by fate to bring about a reconciliation with England. That was perhaps the reason why he flew to England. The 'truth' of this horoscope is equally as well-known as Hitler's.

And what is the position of astrology today? One has to distinguish between a supposedly scientific form, which for instance Alfred Rosenberg (Signs in the Sky) advocates, and a popular form, the so-called solstitial point horoscope. This mentally contagious habit is so widespread, that the large daily newspapers and magazines have to take it into account. We are told that in the United States some 170 newspapers and magazines carry daily horoscopes. It is also known that there are about 25,000 well-paid astrologers in the world today.

A humorous example will give us an insight into the situation.

Ex. 2. I attended a conference of Protestant ministers to which the publishers of certain large newspapers and many other journalists were invited. The discussion was concerning the intellectual level and outlook on life of the newspapers. A minister pointed out that Swedish newspapers contain no horoscopes, and that this is the accepted practice in Sweden. Why was is not possible to adopt the same attitude throughout Germany and other countries? The following explanation was given by the chief editor of a large daily paper. He said that personally he was convinced of the nonsense of astrology, but it was a question of finance. The paper that includes no weekly horoscope in its Sunday edition must count on many cancellations. No newspaper can afford this. He went on to tell of a humorous experience. One Friday the astrologer's horoscope did not arrive on time. In his dilemma he went to a storage room and picked out an old horoscope. Since he did not know the order of the Zodiac, it was an incorrect one. In spite of this, none of the readers noticed the mistake. Since all went well, he saved himself the astrologer's fee, and on 22 occasions he used incorrect horoscopes from previous years. None of the hundreds of thousands of readers noticed this, till finally someone wrote in, saying that it was impossible for the sign of Scorpion to rule in July. Now his trick was uncovered. He had to turn again to the 'experts' for help. Having told his story, the editor then added with a smile, "During the time of the incorrect horoscopes everything went well. It does not depend on the horoscope, but on what the people believe."

What reasons do we have as Christians for not recognizing astrology as being providential to our lives and destinies? First of all we should be repelled by its heathen background. With ancient people astrology had a religious accent. The stars were equivalent to gods. The heathen felt themselves to be led, influenced and threatened by these planet gods, and though, in the course of time, the religious character of astrology receded, the old rules were retained.

Here we have a second reason for rejecting it. The retention of these old rules involves an insoluble contradiction. Every 26,000 years the axis of the earth prescribes the lateral area of a cone (precession). Today's astrologer does not see the planets in the same position as his colleague of 4000 to 5000 years ago. Besides, several other planets have been discovered; Uranus in 1781, Neptune in 1839, and Pluto in 1932. Since all these changes failed to shake the astrological system in any way, present astronomers reject astrology as one of the greatest frauds of all time.

But there are still more impossibilities to be considered. The rays from the stars falling on a child at the moment of birth are said to be decisive to its fate. But this assertion leads to several contradictions. Our earth is being showered predominantly by light and cosmic rays. Yet neither of these has its source in the planets, which of themselves emit no light of their own. The source of the light is found rather in the fixed stars, while cosmic rays originate in the Milky Way. The planets, like our earth, radiate neither of these.

Moreover, the moment when the umbilical cord is cut should be of decisive importance. Thus if a doctor delays the cutting of the cord, the child should receive a different fate. Therefore one ought to consult an astrologer to determine the most favourable time for the doctor to cut the cord. And so the next question is why the 240 people whose cords are cut at the same moment do not have the same fate. Why was there only one Shakespeare, and only one Johann Sebastian Bach, among the many that were born at the same moment in time as they were? Ironically, however, Abbé Moritz Warburg, who is a well-known research worker in astrology, has said, "Astrology just cannot be discredited."

A reform movement in astrology wants to clear away these difficulties. It is called Cosmo-Biology, and its headquarters are in Aalen, Wuerttemberg. Man's heredity must be considered together with the stars, they say. This is but a compromise between the old astrology and modern biology.

Of course there is no question that in some ways the planets do affect our earth. The tides and other natural phenomena are caused or affected by them. But to suggest that these effects influence our lives and destinies would be the same as asserting that the luminous dials of our wrist watches could cause our death through radioactivity.

Yet the main problem we are concerned with in astrology is its effects as we meet them in Christian counselling. It can be stated in three words: Deceit, Suggestion, Occultism. I will give an example of each from my own work.

Ex. 3. A student of psychology at the Sorbonne University in Paris wanted to write his thesis. He put a classified advertisement in a newspaper and passed himself off as an astrologer. For a prepaid fee of 20 francs (30/-) he would cast a detailed horoscope for each applicant. He received about 400 customers and was thus able to finance his own studies. He gave the same horoscope to all 400 customers, paying no heed to the signs of the Zodiac. His only consideration was the psychological aspect: telling everyone that a good future lay ahead of them, and implying positive character traits in everyone, for people like to believe such things and hence would not regret having paid the fee. He received many letters of appreciation, since the horoscope covered almost everybody's situation. The student then wrote his dissertation and passed his degree with honours. In this case the astrology was mere deception. The young Frenchman earned a lot of money and got his degree through the stupidity and superstition of his fellow-men.

Ex. 4. I met the most absurd example of the horoscope disease in the person of a young theologian. As a young man this minister had been a business man. He had had a detailed horoscope cast, in which it was said he would change his profession three times. The young man did not have to be told twice. He attended evening school, and then studied Protestant theology, and was later ordained as a minister. He married, but fortunately had no children. The reason why this was fortunate will soon appear. After a few years he was converted to the Catholic faith, and was received by them as a priest. His wife was allowed to stay with him as his housekeeper. Already two changes were behind him. Today he explains that he has not as yet reached his last station in life. He feels an urge to enter a fourth profession. His plans have yet to be fulfilled. It will not be very long before the change will have taken place. In this case, the unfortunate man has become the victim of suggestion. He lives out his own horoscope. He stands bound and compelled by this astrological prediction.

Ex. 5. A minister who saw his mission as fighting superstition had a horoscope cast for the sake of study. He wanted to prove that horoscope casting was just superstition and deceit. He had to pay a large fee because a detailed horoscope was cast for him. He now waited confidently, believing that the horoscope would not fulfill itself. But he was amazed to see that the prophecies were fulfilled. For eight years he observed that all the predictions came true, even to the smallest details. He grew uneasy at this and reflected on the problem. It had indeed been his preconceived idea that it was all based on suggestion and superstition. Yet he knew that as a Christian he had not been the victim of suggestion. Finally he saw no other way of escape than to repent and to ask God for His protection. The thought came to him that he had sinned through this experiment, and had placed himself under the influence of the powers of darkness. After his repentance he discovered to his surprise that his horoscope was now no longer correct. Through this experience the minister clearly understood that demonic powers can be active in astrology. The person who exposes himself to this danger can perish by it.

How do the experts in various fields judge astrology? Medicine already recognizes the damage that can be done by astrology. The medical superintendent of Wiesbaden, Dr. Schrank, writes in an article about the psychology of superstition, "We can see how dangerous astrology is by the way it produces serious psychic disturbances, a fear of life, despair and other disorders in sensitive people. Astrology paralyses initiative and powers of judgment. It stupefies and encourages shallowness. It moulds the personality into receiving an underground movement that thrives on platitudes."

Astrologers themselves have put it even more clearly. The leading astrologer Wehrle designates astrology as mantic, that is, the art of fortune-telling. Thus in astrology we are faced in part with an occult tendency, together with all the side-effects that occult things carry with them.

The Bible makes it most clear what one's attitude should be towards astrology. In Deuteronomy 17 : 2–5 it is commanded, "If there be found a man or a woman who has gone and served or worshipped the sun or the moon or any of the host of heaven, thou shalt stone that man or woman to death with stones." The prophet Isaiah speaks in even more detail about astrology. He writes in

Isaiah 47 : 13—14, "You are wearied with your many counsels; let them stand forth and save you, those who divide the heavens, who gaze at the stars, who at the new moons predict what shall befall you. Behold they are like stubble, the fire consumes them; they cannot deliver themselves from the power of the flame."

According to the Bible, astrology is to be equated with pagan idol worship, blasphemy, and apostasy from the living God. The second commandment is forgotten by those who deal with it: "Thou shalt not make unto thyself any graven image, or any likeness of anything that is in heaven above, or that is in the earth beneath, or that is in the water under the earth."

(II) Cartomancy

Historically, the use of cards in fortune-telling can be traced back over many centuries. The Romans already possessed a system of small tablets with inscribed symbols. Then in the 8th century, cards appeared. The technique of fortune-telling by means of cards is very simple. Certain cards have certain meanings. For instance the 7 of hearts is the card of love; the 10 of hearts means a wish fulfilled; the 10 of spades is a lucky card; etc. With 52 playing cards there are thousands of combinations. Now let us acquaint ourselves with the main problems of card-laying by means of a few examples.

Ex. 6. An evangelist of the German Tent Mission gave a lecture in which he spoke against fortune-telling and card-laying. Afterwards a church official who had been present called the evangelist over and asked him, "What do you mean by your protest about card-laying? I do it myself. It's a harmless social pastime." We can add a similar example to this from Switzerland.

Ex. 7. A Swiss minister held a bazaar. In the parish

hall several fairy-tale booths were erected. One of the booths had the title 'Fortunes Told'. For about 4d. the children could go in and have their fortunes told by a woman fortune-teller. One of the church elders was annoyed by this and spoke with the minister. "It's a harmless joke", was the only reply. However, a boy who went into this ecclesiastical fortune-telling booth was told that he would have an accident on his bicycle in the following week. Several days later this actually happened, and the boy broke his leg. A girl was told, "Your teacher does not like you." Subsequently the girl suffered much from this alleged dislike of her teacher.

These first two examples show that card-laying cannot be said to be harmless. The two children became the victims of suggestion. The two ministers were the victims of the rationalistic theory of their university education, which leaves a disastrous gap in the field of magic (the mastery of matter through the mind or the soul) and mantic (the art of fortune-telling).

If card-laying is not just concerned with making easy money but does in fact involve paranormal abilities, then telepathy (the reading of thoughts etc.) and subconscious communication will play a part in it. An example should make this clear.

Ex. 8. A sixteen year old girl went to a card-laying fortune-teller. She wanted to know how long she would have to wait till she met her future husband. The woman looked at her closely and said, "Your brother had a serious motorcycle accident a year ago. Is that true?" "Yes", replied the girl. "Your mother has heart trouble. Is that true?" Again "Yes". "At present you are not getting on well with your father. Is that true?" "Yes, but how do you know all this?" "From the cards." In reality the woman possessed the rare ability of telepathy and therefore had read these statements from the girl. By now though, the young client had come to trust the fortune-teller completely, so the woman now went on to tell her about the future. The girl believed the ambiguous statements and inwardly set her mind on their fulfilment. In her superstition she fell victim to a fulfilment compulsion. It was as the Bible says, "According to your faith be it done unto you." The accurate recounting of the past triggered off the psychological process of fulfilment through the subconscious.

Another form of card-laying is based on genuine mediumistic abilities. The word 'mediumistic' comes from the Latin word 'medium' (middle). By 'mediumistic' one means the mysterious ability of some people to describe or to explain certain events in a way that seems to be beyond the range of the five senses. The following case of a woman card-layer should show us the meaning of the word.

Ex. 9. On being questioned, a fortune-teller said that while she was actually in the process of fortune-telling, she was controlled by a strange power. This spirit would come over her and she was then forced to say things of which she had no previous knowledge. It was a feeling as if she was possessed, but after the fortune-telling she was completely normal again.

This example is close to that which is described in Acts 16 : 16—18. Paul was on a missionary journey at Philippi. A girl with the spirit of divination followed him daily. She was continually crying out, "These men are servants of the Most High God, who proclaim to you the way of salvation." Why was Paul unhappy with this statement? Why did he restrain her? The answer is that the apostle saw immediately that the power of fortune-telling at work in the girl was not of God. He turned on the girl and commanded, "In the name of Jesus Christ, come out of her." Immediately the girl was freed of her powers of divination and fortune-telling. This incident in the early missionary work of the Church is very enlightening.

First of all we learn that there are genuine powers of fortune-telling and that it is at least not all fake. The girl had told the truth. She had received her knowledge from other than human intelligences, from demonic powers. Furthermore it becomes clear that fortune-telling can also have a religious flavour. Only too often the occult world camouflages itself with Christian trimmings. The apostle however, at once recognized the source of this power of divination. He had the gift of the discerning of spirits. His spiritual authority as one of Christ's representatives and missionaries showed itself. The name of Jesus was and is equal to all the powers of the world of darkness. The complete victory of the gospel over the demon-bound pagan world was portrayed. In the name of Jesus the chains and fetters broke; the poor oppressed human being was set free. The many factors revealed in this story appear again and again in various forms in the area of fortune-telling.

Christian counselling is not so much concerned with the scientific issues as with the effects that fortune-telling has on people, and the way to overcome these effects. Several examples will clarify this.

Ex. 10. During a counselling session a student confessed that she had several psychic disturbances. She suffered from a fear of examinations, had symptoms of paralysis and no powers of concentration. It appeared as if her intellectual and emotional faculties were completely divided. On being questioned she admitted that she had often had her fortune told from cards. Her parents and grandparents had also sought the advice of fortune-tellers.

Ex. 11. For many years a Christian university graduate practised card-laying for himself, his family, and for fellow members of his church. After his death his wife became an alcoholic. Her whole pension was used on drink. Her house was decorated by a host of bottles. In addition to this the woman started to engage in white magic and thus continued in the occult tradition of her husband. The daughter in turn followed in the footsteps of her parents. She too was caught up in the superstitious customs of her mother. When the girl was seventeen years old, she became mentally ill and was committed to an asylum. Magic and superstition had destroyed the whole family.

Ex. 12. A young Christian man told me of his time in the services. He had been a corporal in a unit where the staff sergeant had laid cards for all the NCO's. At first the corporal had objected to the fortune-telling but finally he gave in to his superior. The card-layer prophesied that he would receive news of a death the following day, and that he could also expect a money-order in the near future. As a matter of fact, the next day he heard that his uncle had died, and five days later he also received the predicted money. The parents had never been in the habit of sending their son money. It was a unique event. After this session with the card-layer, the corporal experienced depressions and his prayer life was disrupted. He had then gone to a Christian man for help and after the man had prayed and laid hands on him, the serious emotional disturbances disappeared completely.

These examples involve a number of problems. The simplest group of questions are of a parapsychological or psychological nature, parapsychology being the science of the extrasensory border experiences of life. Did the staff sergeant possess genuine abilities of fortune-telling? This is not self-evident in the above example. The corporal could have known of the serious illness of his uncle, and he could also have toyed with the idea of his parents sending him some money as a congratulatory gift for his recent promotion. The staff sergeant would then have only needed the help of extrasensory perception, or some telepathic faculty, to have tapped the information from the corporal. This does not seem at all like a case of genuine prevision.

The second group of questions are of a medical character. Were the disturbances caused or triggered off by the fortune-telling, or was it not rather a latent emotional or even mental illness that came to the surface at the time of the fortune-telling experience? Could the coincidence be mistaken for the cause? Has the cause been mistaken for the effect? These are the objections that are always being raised by psychiatry — the science of mental and emotional illnesses. Behind these medical objections are weighty biblical and theological problems. Many doctors and theologians contest the idea that occult practices can evoke psychic and nervous disturbances, and damage to a person's faith. And further back again is the question as to whether there really are other worldly or demonic powers whose effects touch upon human life. In this connection psychiatrists, almost without exception, view the New Testament reports of possessed people as serious cases of hysteria. Many theologians follow this line, and speak of possession as a disease or defect. There are some who have been unable to rid themselves of the rationalistic egg-shells of their liberal theology. Among these one finds in particular all the adherents to Bultmann's theology. They miss the true facts of the biblical accounts entirely. They have no organ of receptivity to the happenings of the Scriptures. Spiritual whoredom with the philosophical trends of the past and present has blunted them against the Holy Spirit. It is indeed embarrassing, when even a positive theologian from Basle, who develops good New Testament thoughts in her booklet 'Salvation and Healing', goes on to call the ability of fortune-telling merely a defect. This is the result and influence of psychiatric doubts. Although there are what one might call defects or illnesses that are recorded as being healed in the New Testament, those possessed by devils are also delivered through the name of the Lord Jesus. The young woman at Philippi with the spirit of divination had no defect, but a demonic spirit. Paul therefore did not heal her by laying his hands on her and praying, but he commanded the unclean spirit to come out of her in the name of Jesus. The particular therapy that Jesus and his disciples used made it clear what the patient was suffering from. To the physically sick, laying on of hands and prayer was applied, while the unclean spirits and demons were met with authority and with the command to come out.

If we return now to the medical questions, we see that the view of the Bible is at variance with the view of modern psychiatry. Medicine must however concede that many mental illnesses do have a magical factor. This is apparent in conversation with many schizophrenics who assert that they are either magically persecuted or bewitched. We must not miss the fact that in many cases magic is the primary cause, and psychic disturbances are the effects and consequences. 20,000 carefully examined cases cannot be disregarded lightly. Besides this, our parapsychologists, as for example Dr. Bender of the University of Freiburg, know of diseases which have arisen after occult practices. Mediumistic psychosis needs to be mentioned only as one example. Christian counselling clearly reveals that spiritistic, magic or fortune-telling activities trigger off disturbances, which can often be proved medically. Moreover in almost every case the faith of the person involved can be seen to be damaged. This indicates that the origin of the damage is primarily of a spiritual nature, as the Scriptures would have us know. For the treatment, then, the minister who as a Christian believes in the Bible is the most qualified. Second to him would be a believing psychiatrist.

(III) Palmistry

To avoid confusion we must clarify what we mean by some of the terms. It is with chiromancy that we will be dealing, and by that is meant the telling of fortunes from the lines of the hand. We will not be considering chirology, the scientific interpretation of the shape and the lines of the hand, nor graphology, the interpretation of handwriting.

Palmistry can be traced back to ancient Rome. Early astrological ideas were mixed up with palmistry. Besides the four main lines, the heart, head, life and fate lines, the palm was divided into seven planetary mounds. From the index finger to the little finger they are the Mercury, Apollo, Saturn and Jupiter mounds.

We will again lead into the question of Christian counselling by means of a few examples. Whereas it was mentioned above that chiromancy, chirology and graphology should be dealt with under separate headings, in practice a disastrous merging of the three takes place. The following is an example of this.

Ex. 13. A young girl went to a graphologist and had her handwriting and her hand lines interpreted. In the written forecast it was stated that she would be murdered in her 30th year. Thereupon the girl told her family, "If I have to die so young, I want to enjoy my life to the full." She engaged in prostitution and had several abortions. Because of her dissolute life she became seriously ill in her 24th year and died of an ulcerated colitis. The doctor stated that she had ruined herself through her licentious living. It should be noted that after the sessions with the graphologist, mediumistic abilities had appeared in the girl. She developed the ability to use a pendulum and a divining rod.

The example reveals first of all that this particular

graphologist used occult methods. He was misusing graphology for the purpose of fortune-telling. One of the most usual forms of fortune-telling is also brought to light by this example, and that is suggestive fortune-telling. There are many forms of this in which the person who has been advised brings about the fulfilment himself, either consciously or subconsciously. This is a repetition of what has been said about the psychological process of card-laying. With regards to Christian counselling, it is frequently observed that fortune-telling causes people to lose all moral inhibitions. Christian education, tradition and custom have built up a protective wall around our lives, and even the person who is far from Christ lives unconsciously in a Christian world order, although he may rebel against it inwardly. Coming to grips with occult powers tears down these walls. Dark, turbid waters stream unhindered into the abandoned life. In the above example the sensual life of the girl gained the upper hand and she was ruined by it. Occultism tends to stir up all one's passions and addictions. A person who has sought advice in the occult field can become irritable, and can abandon himself to alcohol, nicotine and licentious living.

The effects of suggestion in fortune-telling can be further illustrated in the following examples.

Ex. 14. A young woman had her fortune told through palmistry. The fortune-teller informed her that in her 40th year she would die of cancer. As it happens the woman is wasting away already because of this suggestion, and she now lives under the delusion that she is going to have cancer. She has already lost 30 lb and today weighs only six stone.

Ex. 15. The cousin of one of my class-mates was working as a maid in a manse. One day a gipsy woman appeared at the door selling household articles. The girl refused to buy anything because the articles were so dear.

Thereupon the gipsy snatched her hand in order to tell her fortune. The girl wanted to pull her hand away, but the sly woman used a psychological trick. She said quickly, "Oh, that's interesting. You will marry within two years." What girl would refuse to listen when marriage is mentioned? She now willingly let the gipsy read her hand. The woman continued with her prophecy. "Several men will ask you to marry them. You will marry the tallest one. In the first year of your marriage you will become a mother. But I see your life line stops quite suddenly. You will die during the birth of your first child!"

Before going on I will briefly point out the character of this particular piece of fortune-telling. One certainly needs no prophetic ability to say that a pretty girl will marry soon. It is also not necessary to be a prophet to say that she would give birth to a child in the first year of her marriage. Also the reference to death at the end of the piece of fortune-telling was no more than an act of vengeance on the part of the gipsy because the girl had bought nothing from her. But did the words of the gipsy come true?

It so happened that several suitors did appear in the following two years. The girl was already under the influence of the prophecy, and she consequently married the tallest one. During the first year of their marriage she became pregnant. As the time of delivery grew closer her fear increased proportionally. She struggled against the evil prophecy. Her relatives and especially her husband tried to persuade her not to believe the nonsense. But they were unsuccessful. The young woman did not have a strong enough faith to counteract the superstition. She had a normal delivery, but several days later she developed a high fever. The doctor could find no organic cause for this fever at all. Three weeks after the birth of the child the mother became mentally deranged. She was taken to a psychiatric clinic, where she died three days later.

Only those unfamiliar with the psychology of fortune-telling will speak of this as genuine prophecy. In all probability it was only suggestion. We know from the mission fields that the heathen natives are in complete subjection to the 'prophecies' of their medicine men and witch-doctors. If a tribal magician predicts the death of a member of the tribe, then the prediction is soon fulfilled. This is called the psychological phenomenon of thanatomania, the death wish. Death by suggestion exists not only among primitive people, but also among civilized Europeans. In this connection, the Americans have made experiments on convicts that have produced positive results. A man who had been sentenced to death was blindfolded. He was then told that he was to die by having the main artery of his neck opened and that in one minute he would be dead. The skin of his neck was superficially scratched, and at the same time a water tap was turned on near by. The convict felt the cut and heard the water pouring out. Within a minute he had lost consciousness. The experiment had been a success!

With regards to the content of fortune-telling and the form of the prophecies, Professor Zucker in his 'Psychology of Superstition' distinguishes between magical superstition, mystical superstition and thirdly, presentiment. Magical superstition is active. It puts into operation suggestive and magical powers. It interferes decisively and formatively in the life of the one who seeks advice. Almost all the examples given so far fall into this category. Mystical superstition has an intuitive and an adaptive character. It is based on insight, meditation and sensitivity. To it belong the abilities of unification, perception, accommodation and assimilation. The principle behind magical superstition is that the ego gains mastery over the world, while in the case of mystical superstition the ego is said to become merged with the world. The basic difference between these two is in their said method of perception. It is said that prevision may be explained in two ways. Either man carries his whole future within himself in embryo and the information is tapped from this source, or it is supposed that the whole history and destiny of the human race is carried in a kind of world consciousness. This is the opinion held by Professor Osty, E. von Hartmann and Professor Driesch. Mediums are supposed to be able to tap this world consciousness. Both views are based in a certain way on determinism and predestination. From the standpoint of the Scriptures neither of these two methods of fortune-telling are acceptable. To presentiment, the third form of fortune-telling, belong the unconscious premonitions, monitions, veridical dreams, experiences of second sight, clairvoyance, and in fact all the effects of mediumistic abilities. A good example of this is to be found in the book 'Christian Counselling and Occultism' (p 69, Ex. 37). I will not be repeating it here, so as to avoid any overlap in the two publications.

No matter how interesting these scientific distinctions may be, the needs of pastoral work are of far greater importance. We must learn how to help those people who are both emotionally and mentally disturbed, and yet whose symptoms do not fit into the psychiatric picture. To illustrate the effects of palmistry further, I will add two more examples.

Ex. 16. There was a woman who was a fortune-teller, and rejected everything to do with the idea of God. One day a Christian girl was introduced to her. When the girl heard about the woman's strange business of fortune-telling, as a joke she held out her hand. She thought that there was nothing in it. The woman read her palm. The girl laughed and could not stop herself making a facetious remark. However, afterwards the Christian girl suffered from depressions and lost her faith. The fortune-teller's children also exhibited the typical effects. They were all neurotics, living immoral lives. As I said, here we see the typical characteristics of the effects: depression and loss of moral inhibition.

Ex. 17. For many years a man was actively engaged in palmistry. In addition to this he practised mesmerism. Over the years he was himself able to feel the destructive influence of his dubious occupation. He later wanted to become a Christian and for several months forced himself to read the Bible, although he felt a strong inner resistance to this. Every time he faced up to the things of God he felt this strange inward defensiveness and resisting pressure on himself.

A new aspect comes to light in this example. Fortune-telling develops the phenomenon of a resistance and an inner defensiveness towards anything to do with God and His Spirit. When a person who has engaged in fortune-telling wants to come to Christ, he finds the way very difficult. Violent and sinister defensive forces appear, which attempt to prevent a decision for Christ. The person who has been infected and 'immunized' by fortune-telling is almost insensitive to the Holy Spirit. Such people find it very difficult to become Christians.

(IV) Divining with a Rod or Pendulum

As with the case of many other occult practices, people have attempted to make the use of a pendulum scientifically acceptable. The idea of radiaesthesis has been evolved which asserts that all matter radiates. The dowser or pendulum practitioner is supposed to be able to attune himself to this radiation. The scientific aspect of this problem is discussed in 'Christian Counselling and Occultism' (p 81 f). We will again only concern ourselves here with the practical questions which arise in the field of Christian counselling. For the sake of those unacquainted with this phenomenon, it must be pointed out that the use of both a divining rod and a pendulum is basically the same. The only difference is said to be that a pendulum is the more delicate indicator. To make it possible to judge the problem objectively, we will begin with some examples which apparently produced no ill-effects on those involved.

There are doctors, ministers, missionaries and engineers who are convinced of the usefulness and exactness of the results obtained through the use of a rod or pendulum. They say that apart from a certain draining of one's nervous energy there are no derogatory effects.

Ex. 18. A man, 28 years old, committed suicide. Since he just disappeared, a police search was begun to find him. His brother-in-law consulted a pendulum practitioner. The practitioner asked for an object belonging to the missing man, and he was given some socks. Putting these on the floor, he walked around them in rectangle, holding a metal rod. Having done this he was then able to identify the missing man, stating his name, date of birth and the place where he could be found. Then in addition to this, he took a map and a pendulum to check his own statement as to where the man could be found. And the pendulum did just that. The brother-in-law went to the specified place with the police, and they in fact found the body of the man there in a small hut in the forest, where he had shot himself.

Ex. 19. A doctor from Alsace is a dowser. He considers this ability to be a gift of God. It is worth noting, though, that he has a defensive attitude towards the things of God, and is very nervous.

Ex. 20. A postal employee has the ability to find water when using a divining rod or a pendulum, and he can also correctly identify the position of telephone cables with a pendulum. He has commented, however, on signs of tiredness appearing after his dowsing.

Ex. 21. Another doctor had a house built for himself. He wanted to have a well in his garden. A friend of his, a Protestant minister, heard about this. He asked the doctor to give him a plan of the house and garden. He then took a pendulum and established from the plan where water was to be found. His findings were correct, and water was found after digging at the prescribed spot.

Ex. 22. A missionary using a pendulum on the second floor of a house, had the ability to tell whether or not someone was on the floor below him, and to determine whether it was a man or a woman. If it was a woman he could also determine whether she was pregnant or not, and if so, whether the child would be a boy or a girl. He often did such experiments in the presence of his friends, and they were always successful. In the same way he could go to a cemetery and determine whether any particular grave was that of a man or a woman. Obviously when doing this experiment he did not look at the name on the gravestone.

Ex. 23. A Salvation Army officer was a pendulum practitioner for many years. During the war, when his son was missing, he used a pendulum over his son's photograph to determine whether he was alive or not. Once after the war, when his suitcase was stolen, he used his pendulum to discover where the stolen suitcase was. The pendulum directed him to the right place. In reply to my question if he had suffered any ill-effects from his pendulum practice, he replied in the negative, saying that as far as he was concerned he had felt no damage had been done to his Christian life.

Glancing quickly at these six examples we find ourselves already furnished with a few clues which will help us formulate an opinion on the matter. First of all it becomes clear that these things cannot be explained away as mere nonsense. There are in existence both dowsers and pendulum practitioners who can make exact predictions, even though many geologists and other scientists argue strongly to the contrary. But it must also be borne in mind that many of the statements which arise from the use of a pendulum do contain only confused, muddled and irrelevant information.

It also becomes obvious from the few examples just mentioned that many people support the use of a rod or pendulum. A doctor, a minister, a missionary and others have been cited as having indulged in this practice. Who is right, then? Those who fanatically support the idea, or those who passionately oppose it? Either way it would be very wrong to argue that if ministers and other such people use a pendulum, then it must be harmless. It is obvious that adultery is not justified because we may know of a missionary who has committed adultery! So too one can reject the following argument: if some supposedly Christian people feel no derogatory effects after using a pendulum, then instances where the opposite is true cannot be taken seriously. It is true that I do know of several cases where dowsing with a divining rod has apparently had no ill-effects on the dowser. But it must not be forgotten that effects can also lie dormant. With some people the cloven hoof may only reveal itself at their deathbed, or maybe at a time when the person wants to become a Christian. We must also free ourselves from the idea that everyone who proclaims the Word of God is a real Christian. The words of the Bible are still applicable: "They say, 'Thus says the Lord', when the Lord has not sent them" (Ezek. 13:6). A minister using a pendulum can be burdened as much as anyone belonging to any other profession. In my work I have had ample evidence to the effect that the Catholic priest Emmenegger, by using a pendulum on his patients, has been the cause of serious burdening to many of them. Not long ago a Protestant minister was tried and convicted on account of some bad mistakes that he had made when using a pendulum in treating people.

It is a fatal mistake to confuse the ability to use a pendulum with a gift of God. The doctor from Alsace is not the only one to do this. Many pastors and ministers share his view. But which view should we take? On examining many family histories one finds that the ability to use a rod or a pendulum, together with mesmerism, clairvoyance, second sight and veridical dreams, occur in people whose ancestors include active spiritists or maybe a magic charmer. These unusual human abilities are not gifts of the Spirit, nor even neutral or natural gifts, but are rather mediumistic abilities. Many people possess these abilities unknowingly. Sometimes they are detected accidentally. Now and again it happens that a person possessing mediumistic abilities is saved and becomes a Christian. Then suddenly as a Christian he may discover his extraordinary ability and so form the idea that he has a gift of the Spirit. And this is of course untrue. In pastoral work one notices that sometimes these mediumistic abilities disappear when the person is converted, but they are often dragged into the person's new life. Yet a Christian who prays earnestly to be delivered from these abilities will have his prayer answered. Many Christians do in fact find these abilities a burden to them. Markus Hauser said that clairvoyance was not so much a gift but a plague to him. These mediumistic abilities must never be regarded as gifts of the Spirit. Mediumistic abilities are not even sanctified through conversion. Things acquired by one's ancestors in the service of Satan will never be used or sanctioned later on by the Holy Spirit.

The relationship between the use of a pendulum and mediumistic powers can be clarified by means of two examples.

Ex. 24. A young man was treated for a disease by a nature healer who also used a pendulum and practised magic charming. After the treatment the patient developed mediumistic abilities. He suddenly became clairvoyant and at the same time was able to use mental suggestion over a distance.

Ex. 25. After the war a woman gave a photograph of her missing husband to a pendulum practitioner to discover where he was. She afterwards experienced symptoms of clairvoyance. She had somnambulistic experiences, and found that she could as it were send her soul out over great distances. In this plight she sought the help of a minister, and having repented and surrendered her life to Christ the mediumistic abilities disappeared.

There are also both conscious and unconscious transferences of mediumistic abilities. Through the treatment of a highly mediumistic occultist, the patient can easily become mediumistic himself. We have here the demonic counterpart to the laying on of hands of the disciples in the Acts of the Apostles. Through the apostles' laying on of hands some Christians received the gift of the Holy Spirit (Acts 8:17, 19:6). There is also a conscious form of transference connected with dowsers and pendulum practitioners. In counselling, many people have said that they received their sensitivity to use a divining rod, when a strong dowser had held their hands while searching for water. The rod had suddenly reacted and this mediumistic ability had remained with them afterwards.

The following examples, better than any amount of theoretical explanation, will give us an insight into the important difference between mediumistic abilities and the spiritual powers referred to in the Bible.

Ex. 26. A woman who had an organic disease went to be examined by a pendulum practitioner. A diagnosis was made and the medical treatment was prescribed through the use of a pendulum. The woman, who had a Christian outlook and attitude, afterwards felt as though she was being approached by unearthly forces. These strange assaults lasted for a few months. During this time she sought the help of a Christian minister because of the strange inner fear that gripped her.

Ex. 27. Since childhood a girl had had the gift of second sight. She often saw apparitions. She was also antagonistic towards religious matters. However, during a mission she accepted Christ as her Saviour. From that time on her resistance to the things of God was gone. But one day she fell ill and unknowingly went to a pendulum practitioner. Immediately her psychic disturbances and her resistance to the Bible and prayer returned.

This example underlines the following facts. It has been said earlier that the gift of second sight is one of the subsequent effects of the occult activities of one's ancestors. Another common symptom of this is a resistance to things concerning religion. The girl in Ex. 27 had both these symptoms. When she turned to Christ the mediumistic subjection departed. After the pendulum treatment they both reappeared. Here the mediumistic character of the pendulum practice becomes apparent. This characteristic resistance which accompanies other symptoms will be seen more clearly through some further examples.

Ex. 28. During an illness a woman sought the help of a well-known pendulum practitioner. She thought nothing of doing this, as she had previously heard nothing against such a practice. However, she became restless in the waiting room of the practitioner and this unrest increased during the treatment itself. She took the medicines which had been prescribed by the pendulum but the degree of her psychic disturbances only intensified. She found it impossible to pray and developed an aversion to the Bible and to the things of her faith. It was then on her own initiative that she threw away the medicines. Only after this did she come to seek my advice as a minister, and to ask me what I thought about the use of a pendulum in diagnosing diseases and in prescribing medicines.

Ex. 29. A pendulum practitioner came to me. He admitted quite openly that his practice was a strain on him and consumed his nervous energy. He specialized in determining the constituency of foods by means of a pendulum. White sugar he said would affect him negatively, while brown sugar would do so positively. Over the years, however, he had observed psychic changes in himself. He had suffered a loss of energy and a loss in his ability to make decisions. Added to this he had become hypersensitive, and had developed a nervous twitching and a sensitivity to southerly winds and to water. When he tried to read the Bible, he had a feeling of disgust and a great aversion towards it. Crucifixes were also violently repugnant to him. All this he observed in himself, and realizing that these psycho-religious disturbances were connected with his pendulum practice, he sought pastoral help and found himself ready to surrender his life to Christ.

These two examples show that both the woman and the pendulum practitioner became aware of the derogatory effects through their own sound judgement and insight. In both cases they came to reject the use of a pendulum before ever receiving any such advice from a Christian minister.

The antagonism that exists between mediumistic pendulum practices and the spiritual power of prayer is revealed in the next three examples.

Ex. 30. A well-known dowser was asked one day by a professor of medicine, to walk through the various buildings of the clinic with a divining rod and to note its reactions. The reason for the professor's request was the fact that in one of the buildings belonging to the clinic an exceptionally high rate of deaths occurred. When a seriously ill patient was moved into this building their condition usually worsened. However, the professor did not tell this to the dowser. He wanted to have an unbiased report. The dowser went through the different buildings and actually established that there were stronger impulses in the 'house of death'. The professor, who in fact was very sceptical about the result, nevertheless had some screening put up to counteract the so-called impulses. The result was puzzling. The number of deaths there immediately declined. So as to avoid gossip, the professor is usually silent about this experience.

The dowser in question is not only able to use a divining rod, but is also a clairvoyant. He can for example state where the members of his family are at any time. He is also consulted by insurance companies and real estate agents to determine the condition of building plots. In the course of his activities this dowser and clairvoyant confessed that he was unable to pray. An inner force prevented him from doing so.

Ex. 31. A Christian wanted to discover if there was a spring in his large garden. A dowser had reactions in two places but no water was found on digging there. The dowser was surprised and said, "This has never happened to me before." The Christian man in reply said that he had prayed about the matter beforehand, since he had not been sure whether he as a Christian should have called a dowser in to help or not. "Well, that's why," replied the dowser, "Of course it wouldn't work."

Ex. 32. One pendulum practitioner casts spells over warts, corns, goitres, and eczemas etc. Added to this he experiments in the field of death magic. He also asserts that he can either make people sick or heal them. A Christian woman who knew nothing of his magical powers, thinking that he was only a nature healer, went to him for treatment. In the waiting room she prayed silently. Suddenly he addressed her and said, "You can go home. I can't help you." In spite of this, the woman began to have attacks of depression and thoughts of suicide. Her husband, who had no clear relationship with Christ, was treated magically by this same pendulum practitioner. The children born of their marriage since this treatment have all been affected and burdened. It is also worth noting that a doctor nearby sends some of his patients to this pendulum practitioner.

These three examples indicate that dowsing can paralyse a man's desire to pray, while on the other hand the prayer of a believing Christian can paralyse dowsing. The woman praying in the waiting room prevented the magic pendulum practitioner from working. The power of the Holy Spirit and mediumistic abilities are mutually exclusive.

Finally we will mention the definite effects of using a pendulum. We will be dealing not so much with the effects on one's Christian life but rather with authentic medical disturbances.

Ex. 33. A young man, being out of work, had a pendulum practitioner find jobs for him by using a pendulum over the 'Vacant Jobs' column of a newspaper. In this way he had the offer of five jobs in one day. But although he got a job immediately, after a few days he had to give it up again because he became emotionally disturbed. He then spent some months in a mental hospital. When his health improved he turned to some monks for advice. Again he was told to seek the help of a pendulum practitioner. Finally he sought the counsel of a magic charmer. The result was that a few days later he had attacks of temporary insanity and was again taken to the mental hospital.

Ex. 34. A young man with bronchial asthma was being treated by a pendulum practitioner. Both the diagnosis and the required medicine were determined by the use of a pendulum. Besides working with a pendulum the man was also a magic charmer, and he used the following charm on the young patient: "Blood turn to water, water turn to pus, pus come out." He then put bandages on several parts of the patient's body, after having covered the bandages with salves. A few days later some pus actually formed under the bandages. The pus drained out but the bronchial asthma was not healed. Yet from that time the young man began to have nervous and mental disturbances. He felt that his memory was failing, and he could no longer concentrate on his studies since he felt a numbness in his head. These disturbances caused him to seek the advice of a Christian minister.

Ex. 35. A Protestant minister used a pendulum to find water and ore. He could also diagnose diseases and establish the character of medicines with the pendulum. A Swiss university professor tested his ability. With his medical assistants and students present, he introduced twenty patients to the pendulum practitioner. With the help of the pendulum the man made a correct diagnosis on all 20 patients. This minister was also not immune to the effects of his practice. His wife had a fatal accident. All his children died unnatural deaths. He himself has now been in an asylum for a number of years.

Ex. 36. A minister in Germany used a pendulum in dealing with diseases and medicines. He also practised healing at a distance. Sick people would send him their photographs and he would hold the pendulum over them to find out the medicine that should be prescribed. A believing Christian woman sent him her photograph for the same purpose. Her illness was diagnosed and the necessary medicine determined. However, later on she became insane and was taken to an asylum. Members of her family reported this to the church authorities and the minister was later brought to court.

These four examples reveal a fact that can be verified

by hundreds of similar cases. Pendulum therapy can indeed accomplish a certain relief and healing in the organic field. This organic relief, however, must be paid for by disturbances appearing in the psychic field. Even the minister who was an active pendulum practitioner was not immune. The degree of psychic disorder differs only in this, that the active pendulum practitioner experiences more complicated sicknesses as a result of his mediumistic activity, than the people who are treated. In many cases the occult character of the pendulum practice is revealed by the fact that the pendulum practitioner often indulges in other occult activities. This may include for example magic charming, spiritism, clairvoyance, or mesmerism etc. The company is worthy of note. Birds of a feather flock together!

(V) Mirror Mantic or Crystal Gazing

There are in existence occult text books on the subject of mirror mantic and mirror magic. The mirror magician with the help of a magic mirror may attempt to heal or to persecute through magic, to treat people at a distance or to use love and defence magic, and so on. Mirror mantic is often directed at discovering things unknown to the inquirer, in uncovering crimes or diagnosing difficult diseases, and it can embrace any physical event which happens in the world. Mirrors are not the only occult tools used in this field, but crystal balls, rock crystal and other reflecting objects all play a part. Some even use water as a reflecting surface.

Historically, mirror mantic or crystal gazing can be traced back over hundreds of years. Even the fairy tale with the mirror on the wall contains this theme. Mirror gazing also has a place in mysticism. Jacob Boehme is supposed to have received his best thoughts while meditating over a glass ball, one like those once used by shoemakers to concentrate the light on their work. From the psychological point of view, crystal gazing may aid auto-suggestion or auto-hypnosis, and may help to arouse certain subconscious processes. The indication is that this form of fortune-telling sets into motion forces that are mainly subconscious. Since these subconscious forces are far removed from conscious control, they can easily give entrance to powers outside ourselves. Paul does not say in vain that we wrestle not against flesh and blood, but against the evil spirits of the air (Eph. 6:12). A few examples will again serve as an introduction to this form of fortune-telling.

Ex. 37. A farm owner had a large number of sheep. One day several of the sheep disappeared and no trace could be found of them. The farm boy ran to a crystal gazer who was said to be able to solve and to clear up any problem he was faced with. He asked for his advice. The man went into his small room and stayed there for some time. Finally he reappeared and said, "Go to the first road from the farm, turn right and climb straight up the hill. On the top there is a large rock. The sheep are there." The boy followed this advice and found the sheep.

Ex. 38. A farmer went to a crystal gazer complaining that his cow had been stolen the previous night. Could he say where the cow now was? The fortune-teller went into his room and concentrated on his mirror. In the end he came out and stated, "Your cow is on Holzerjoerg's farm. She is in fact in the barn behind a number of bales of straw. Take three or four people there together with a policeman. Some of you go into the house and the others go straight to the barn." The man followed this advice and recovered his cow.

Ex. 39. One night the garage containing the car of a non-Christian was burned down. The man assumed it to be arson and he notified the police. The police investigation was unsuccessful. To identify the fire raiser, he then went to someone who practised mirror divination. The clairvoyant retreated into a room for about twenty minutes. When he came out of the semi-darkened room, he held his magic mirror out to the man and said, "This is the person who did it." The man was startled as he recognized his former schoolmate in the mirror. He exclaimed, "It's impossible. We are on very good terms." "The mirror does not lie", said the clairvoyant. As the man left, the clairvoyant added quite casually, "Something else. You will die soon!" The bewildered man then went to see his schoolmate, and confronting him asked, "Did you have anything to do with the burning of my garage?" The schoolmate became quite confused and then admitted his guilt. In reply to questions of motive, he confessed that he was very jealous about his former school-friend's success, since he himself had always suffered setbacks in his own profession. The fire raiser begged his victim to keep quiet about it. He offered to replace the garage and car, which he soon did.

About four weeks later in the middle of the night the garage owner screamed terribly. His wife woke up and turned on the light. She saw her husband writhing in terrible convulsions. She sent for a doctor immediately, and her husband was transferred to the university clinic. There he remained unconscious and had to be fed intravenously for ten days. During this time a church group interceded for him daily. The patient finally regained consciousness and was able to speak about what he had experienced in the previous ten days. When he had originally cried out in the night, he had seen in a dream or half-dream some horrible devilish figures approaching him which had pulled him along on a descent into hell. In the course of this fearful experience all the guilt of his past life had appeared before his eyes. He had also recognized the minute details of the fire, and the session with the clairvoyant had also come to his mind again. The black figures that had dragged him into the dark abyss had explained to him that the measure of his sins was full, and that he now had to be crucified for them. He had then experienced a terrible and painful crucifixion. After horrible mistreatment and seemingly unending torment, these black figures had disappeared again. It had then grown lighter, and then he had regained consciousness. Later he learnt from the doctor that he had been unconscious for ten days. The man completely changed after this experience. Previously he had wanted little to do with things concerning the Bible, but now he began to attend the services and Bible studies of the local church. He became very active, and used to fill his car with neighbours every Sunday to take them to the church.

In spite of all the confused and doubtful statements that do come from many mirror fortune-tellers, these three examples show that some of them can get genuine information from their mirrors. In the first two cases I was not able to follow up the effects. The third example, however, reveals them clearly. I assume though, that the man fell victim to an unconscious suggestion when the fortune-teller casually stated that he would soon die. He was obviously greatly disturbed to hear that his schoolmate had caused the fire. His thoughts were centered on his friend and the ignominious story. At that moment his consciousness was diverted and his subconscious mind was open. It was a good moment for the fortune-teller to make his suggestion, which would then have penetrated the subconscious. The resulting sickness was not true prevision. It would be, to use the terminology of Zucker, not so much a mystical or foreseeing act of fortune-telling, as a magical and inducive fortune-telling act. Such examples are sufficient to warn Christians to avoid all forms of fortune-telling.

(VI) Psychometry

The word psychometry means 'to measure the mind or the soul'. This definition was originally used by the American, Professor Buchanan. It is extremely difficult to describe the essence of psychometry. A few examples may best introduce the subject to us.

Ex. 40. A young man who came to me in my pastoral work, had the strange ability of being able to discover someone's identity and character with the help of some object belonging to the person. I will cite one example of this. One day his family doctor gave him a few lines of handwriting in order to test him. The doctor did not say whose writing it was, yet the boy concentrated on the lines and then stated exactly who the writer was, giving her address, her family background, her diseases and other things. The doctor was able to verify the truth of these statements.

One might ask in this example whether it was not simply telepathy. Maybe this young clairvoyant got his information from the doctor rather than from the handwriting. At best this argument can only be partly correct, for the boy reported things of which the doctor had no knowledge, but which were later discovered to be correct.

Ex. 41. During a mission in Switzerland I met a clairvoyant in my counselling who used psychometric powers, and who could make statements that were 100% accurate. If one were to place before him an object belonging to a patient who was unknown to him, for example a handkerchief, then he was able to identify the disease of that person. A professor in Zurich tested his ability and confirmed that his statements were reliable.

This clairvoyant could do other stunts using his psychometric ability. In much the same way he could state from what diseases people had died. Ex. 18 records another case of psychometry.

The difficult question is how these psychometric powers of clairvoyance come about. Some parapsychologists, for example Richet, Geley, Osty, Price, Gumppenberg, Gatterer, believe that clothing and in fact any object used daily by a person will become impregnated by them in some way or other. The psychometric clairvoyant is supposed to have the ability to grasp and interpret these mental-psychic impressions. This explanation is very questionable when one considers that the psychometric clairvoyant is not only able to uncover the past, but also the future of the person concerned. Here we find ourselves without doubt in the field of mediumistic fortune-telling. This deduction is confirmed when one examines the fate of such psychometrists. In my work I have had the opportunity to examine many psychometric practices. For instance, the clairvoyant in Ex. 40 wanted to come to Christ. Immediately, a state of pronounced resistance developed. Resistance to spiritual things became so strong that when trying to pray his concentration vanished entirely. Afterwards however, his mind was completely clear again. It was not even possible for him to recite a prayer, although he was an intelligent man and wanted to pray. No encouragement from the Word of God was able to penetrate this barrier. During prayer he had spells of fainting. Later I discovered that this psychometrist had also used the dangerous magic book, the 6th and 7th Book of Moses. This would again point to the mediumistic character of psychometry, i. e. its being found in the company of black magic.

There are yet other forms of fortune-telling that could be discussed, as for instance that which is based on the excursion of the psyche or soul. We could also include here the many questions which arise in the area of Christian Science, Theosophy and Anthroposophy. In

'Christian Counselling and Occultism' some twenty forms of fortune-telling are enumerated (p 92). The technique of fortune-telling often changes, but the spirit and the force behind it remains the same.

(VII) The Position of the Bible

The Scriptures are unanimous in their judgement and rejection of fortune-telling. At no period in the history of the children of Israel were fortune-tellers recognized. From the earliest history to the time of Christ and on into the time of the apostles, fortune-telling in all its forms was rejected. The following passages bear witness to this:

"If a person turns to mediums and wizards (astrologers), playing the harlot after them, I will set my face against that person, and will cut him off from among his people." Lev. 20:6.

"A man or a woman who is a medium or a wizard shall be put to death; they shall be stoned with stones, and their blood shall be upon them." Lev. 20:27.

"There shall not be found among you any one who practises divination, a soothsayer, or an augur, or a sorcerer, or a charmer, or a wizard, or a necromancer. For whoever does these things is an abomination to the Lord." Deut. 18:10—12.

This is part of the Law as given to Moses, but the same rule remained valid as we read further in the time of the kings and the prophets:

"So Saul died for his unfaithfulness in that he did not keep the command of the Lord, and also consulted a medium, seeking guidance, and did not seek guidance from the Lord." 1 Chron. 10:13.

"Do not let your diviners who are among you deceive you, and do not listen to the dreams which they dream, for it is a lie which they are prophesying to you in my name; I did not send them, says the Lord." Jer. 29:8, 9.

The same condemnation is found in other passages: 1 Sam. 28:6—21, Is. 8:19, 44:25; Ez. 21:21, Mic. 3:6, 7, Jer. 29:8. We have already discussed the passage in Acts 16:16—18, but in Rev. 21:8 we read, "But as for the cowardly, the faithless, the polluted, as for murderers, fornicators, sorcerers, idolaters and all liars, their lot shall be in the lake that burns with fire and brimstone, which is the second death."

We maintain that in all these passages fortune-telling in both its scientific and its primitive forms stands under the judgement of God. God has given them up! This basically is the reason why so much damage is caused to the bodies and minds of those who come into contact with the many forms of fortune-telling. We will just briefly summarize these effects, although it must be pointed out that the list only represents a frequency pattern, and it cannot be assumed that these effects are always the result of occult practices. Nevertheless people infected or burdened by fortune-telling and occult phenomena very frequently suffer in the following ways:

The characters of such people reveal abnormal passions, instability, violent tempers, addiction to alcohol, nicotine and sexual vices, selfishness, gossiping, egotism, cursing etc.

Their religious lives reveal on the one hand an antagonism towards religion, callousness, scepticism, a vicious critical attitude and an inability to pray or read the Bible if they are an atheistic type of person, while on the other hand the pious type reveals a self-righteousness, a spiritual pride, phariseeism, hypocrisy and an insensitivity to the workings of the Holy Spirit.

Medically speaking the families of those involved in fortune-telling reveal in a remarkable way such things as nervous disturbances, psychopathic and hysteric symptoms, cases of St. Vitus' dance, symptoms of paralysis, epileptics, freaks, deaf-mutes, cases of mediumistic psychoses, and a general tendency towards emotional and mental illnesses etc.

Finally to prevent any fundamental misunderstanding, it must be pointed out that the concepts of fortune-telling and prophecy are not to be confused. God is the source of all true prophecy, while the devil is the source of fortune-telling. Prophecy is inspired by the Holy Spirit but fortune-telling is of demonic inspiration. The girl with the spirit of divination at Philippi was possessed of an evil spirit. The prophet Agabus in Acts 21 was moved by the Holy Spirit. There must be an absolutely clear distinction in our minds between these two concepts.

(VIII) Deliverance

It is possible to be delivered from the influence and the effects of fortune-telling. The apostle Paul's meeting with the girl at Philippi led to her complete and immediate liberation. At the name of Jesus the spirits of darkness are powerless. Christ's victory on the cross at Golgotha reminds us that all the powers of darkness and hell have been broken. The treatment of people affected by fortune-telling is thus not primarily a problem for the psychiatrist, who is only qualified for purely medical matters, but is rather the concern of the Christian counsellor. Basically deliverance is only possible through Jesus Christ. Hence people who are oppressed by fortune-telling must first come to Christ. Leading up to this, one finds that a complete confession of sin is indispensable. Confession in the Bible is a voluntary act. Protestant Christians reject any coercion in this matter. Yet in my ministry I have not found one instance of a person suffering from occult subjection being delivered without the help of confession.

By way of encouragement I will give some examples where deliverance was possible. However, the question is dealt with more fully in my book 'Belastung und Befreiung', and also in the last fifty pages of 'Christian Counselling and Occultism'. We will also return to this subject in the concluding pages of this book.

Ex. 42. A girl from a Christian family worked in a large factory. In her department there was a woman who laid cards for all the girls employed there. The Christian girl hesitated for a long time before joining in with the other girls. Since childhood her mother had warned her against it. Finally, however, her curiosity won and she went to see the woman. The cards were shuffled and dealt out on the table. Suddenly the woman exclaimed abruptly to the girl, "I can't lay cards for you."

Ex. 43. A young woman was being treated magically for an organic disease. The unqualified doctor used a pendulum to determine which medicine to prescribe. One day this magician told her that within a few years she would be paralysed. In fact after a year or so the woman actually developed symptoms of paralysis on the right side of her body. Her arm and part of her leg became insensitive and immovable. At the same time she found it impossible to pray or to read her Bible, and a strange fear took hold of her. After a complete confession, however, I prayed over the woman according to James 5:14. The paralysis disappeared from that moment.

Ex. 44. A woman often visited a fortune-teller and she was also in the habit of consulting a pendulum practitioner. Since she had begun doing this it was as if her house had become haunted. She heard scratching and knocking, and saw shadowy ghostly figures. These experiences were a cause of fear to her and so she sought the advice and help of a minister who was able to lead her to Christ. On becoming a Christian the haunting ceased.

These three examples show the power of faith in Christ. The girl from the Christian family was surrounded by the prayers of her relatives. One experiences quite often that people for whom many others are praying are protected when danger threatens them. The magic power of the occult worker was paralysed in her case. The second example again reveals the suggestive power of fortune-telling. In turning to Christ this woman was delivered from a suggestive spell. In the third example it is not absolutely certain whether the woman actually had authentic, objective ghost experiences. It may have been an hallucination. Either way, though, through her new-found faith in Christ she was freed from these experiences. The next two examples of deliverance concern the two most powerful pendulum practitioners that I have ever met.

Ex. 45. A doctor discovered that he had the ability to use a pendulum. He began a series of experiments that lasted over a period of about a week. When a new patient entered his consulting room, he would first offer him a chair, and then he would go into an adjoining room and use a pendulum over the letters of the alphabet to find out the patient's Christian names, surname and complaint. The results proved to be correct in each case and the successes encouraged the doctor to conduct further experiments. When a nurse called from his branch office and told him of some new patients, he used the same method. With the help of the pendulum and the alphabet he discovered the names, diseases and ages of the still unknown patients. The results always proved to be correct. These surprising successes spurred him on to make yet other more difficult experiments. For instance, if he wanted to know the time of departure or arrival of a train, he found that the pendulum obligingly gave him the desired information. He could also with the help of the pendulum state the names, ages, family relationships and other things of people, merely by using the pendulum in conjunction with a photograph of the individual in question. There appeared to be nothing impossible to this pendulum practitioner.

During these experiments, however, the doctor observed various psychic changes in himself. He lost control of himself sexually as well as towards alcohol and smoking. He often had fits of temper and did not understand why. Already after the first week of experimenting with the pendulum he had felt and feared that he was going out of his mind. After a time he therefore stopped using his pendulum and in his inner confusion he endeavoured to become a Christian. In doing so he was completely delivered from the powers that he had been working with. Today this doctor believes that such pendulum abilities depend on demonic forces, because the characteristic effects appeared not only in his mental life but also in his spiritual life.

Ex. 46. During a missionary conference in Switzerland I met an evangelist whose life story is a triumph of the grace of God. As a young man, after being deceived by his fiancée, he had turned to fortune-telling. Since all the statements of the fortune-teller were fulfilled, he became curious to learn the art for himself. He started using a pendulum at first only to examine food. Soon, however, he turned to more profitable experiments. He used the pendulum to determine the prices of rival businesses, and he was successful in this. Afterwards he had seen a price-list of one of the firms and his results had coincided with it. At night he had influenced his clients using a magic mirror, and in this way he had forced them to give him their orders. Finally he went on to healing. He was able to accurately diagnose illnesses and at the same time he could prescribe the most suitable medicines. Through his magic charming he was able to heal toothache, stop bleeding, cure rheumatism, and treat people even when they were not present, as well as many other things. And added to all this he was able to locate anything that had been lost merely by using his pendulum. Here briefly are two examples.

A transport plane crashed in the mountains. After an unsuccessful search the government offered a reward for its discovery. This man took an atlas and a pendulum and determined that the plane had crashed at the foot of Piz Duan. He reported this but they did not believe him. Later however, the wreckage of the plane was discovered where he had said it would be. On another occasion a skier was lost at Valaise in Switzerland. With the help of a pendulum and a map he located the missing man. The highlights of his pendulum experiments were his predictions. When Germany acquired the Sudeten mountains in 1938 his pendulum predicted that there would be war in 1939. As with many pendulum practitioners he thought that his ability was a gift of God. He also considered his pendulum activities to be a new science.

One day he had a booklet given to him, written by a Christian. He noticed the passage Deut. 18:10–12, "For whoever does these things is an abomination to the Lord." These words hit home. A great inward battle began. He threw away his pendulum literature together with his books on magic, and he tried to free himself from it all. Only now did he realize who he had been serving. He later wrote in a booklet, "The devil, who through my activities had a claim on my soul, beat and tormented me incessantly." He came to a point of complete inner bankruptcy. For many months he fought and battled to be delivered. A prayer group started interceding for him. For 15 months the battle went to and fro. Hours of joy and faith were interspersed with hours of depression. He was still not delivered of his magic. He had yet to give up the idea that his use of a pendulum had nothing to do with science. Only then was the power given to him to break free from all his occult practices. At once the pressure lifted and a great peace entered his life. He had assurance that he had been forgiven. Jesus Christ became the centre of his life and since then he has served his Lord faithfully. During one of my missions in Zurich he gave the closing message entitled "From magician to evangelist". "If the Son shall make you free you shall be free indeed."

We will conclude with an example of how a young man was delivered after he had read of the dangers involved in occult practices.

Ex. 47. A young man with a Christian background learned how to use a pendulum. He thought that it was a new branch of science. Later he became engaged to a Christian girl who called his attention to the dangers of using a pendulum. She gave him Modersohn's book "Under the Spell of the Devil" (Im Banne des Teufels). Through reading this book he recognized that the powers behind such a practice were evil. He tried to free himself from their grip yet he found this impossible and even began to have experiences involving ghosts. His fiancée then started a small prayer group to intercede for him. The battle lasted for about a year, but in the end he was completely delivered through the power of Christ.

Chapter Two

Magic

In this chapter we will again be drawing heavily upon the experiences of pastoral work, and it is our desire that the examples which we shall be quoting will serve both as a warning and as a source of information to Christians who may become involved in this field. Having counselled thousands of people in the course of my ministry I am amazed at the way in which modern man still cleaves to the ancient customs and magic practices of the past, in spite of the present standard of scientific knowledge. If magic were only a harmless superstition, then a warning such as this would not be so urgently needed. But in fact many people are today being psychically ruined through magic. A mission held quite recently revealed this to be the case. The minister had told the elders of the church that if someone was going to be either muddled or confused through the mission, then even if 49 other people were helped by it, he did not want the mission to take place. In spite of this objection, following the unanimous approval of the church elders, the mission was held. As it turned out over a hundred people came to be counselled. These sessions revealed that the whole community was being troubled and burdened by nature healers and unqualified doctors, who relied upon occult methods for their healing successes. Many of the people had thus been treated magically, and suffered daily as a result of this. In the counselling sessions I was constantly being asked, "Why aren't we warned about magic and sorcery from the pulpit?" Here then we have two points of view, that of the local minister and that of the congregation. In seeking to solve this problem we ask the question, "Should 49 people be allowed to suffer through lack of information, for fear of harming the one person by making the information public?" If this argument were followed all propaganda against drug addiction or infectious diseases would have to be curtailed. However, our argument is not the important thing, it is what the Bible says that counts. In Ezek. 3 we read of the commission that was given to Ezekiel to be a watchman. It was his duty to warn the wicked of the evil of their ways. As members of the Body of Christ we have a similar duty.

The watchman's task is a difficult one but it is one that is filled with expectancy and hope. The source of our message is the victory of Christ. The devil and his angels are indeed a terrible reality, yet Christ has triumphed over them, on the cross He robbed them of their power. Therefore those who follow in the steps of Christ stand on victorious ground. All power in heaven and upon earth belongs to our Lord and Saviour Jesus Christ and so we have no reason to fear. It only remains for all those who read these words and who face up to the reality of this subject to set their eyes upon Jesus, and to place their lives in His hands for Him to protect them.

(I) The Concept of Magic

What do we understand by the term magic? The answer to this question depends on the attitude and point of view of the questioner. The psychologist, the doctor, the student of folklore, the philosopher, the occultist, the liberal (de-mythologizing) theologian and the true Christian — to all these magic will appear in a different light. People are sharply divided and opinions range from considering it to be nonsense to it being an addiction. From my experience as a minister I would like to put forward the following definition. Magic is the much disputed art of or at least attempt at knowing and ruling the spirit, human, animal and plant worlds, together with the world of dead matter, through extrasensory means with the aid of the mystical and accompanying ceremonies. Let me briefly explain the various assertions in this definition.

The very existence of magic is strongly contested. Psychiatry sees the question of magic as being the symptom of a mental illness. Psychology would say that when people are subjected to magic it is only the result of an incorrect upbringing, and that such people are superstitiously maladjusted and have a false conception of life. Liberal theology would even, in its modern form, regard magic simply as a system of traditional customs and ideas.

The ethical character of magic is also a battle ground of opinion. Some praise it as a gift of God while others see in it just neutral forces of nature which can be used either for good or for evil. Again others, especially the Christian, know of the demonic character of magic.

Why are events involving magic so difficult to judge? Going back to our definition we see that magic is practised through extrasensory forces being called into play. Our five senses have only a limited range. On the physical level people are ready to admit this, since science furnishes us with ample proof of the existence of areas that are beyond our human senses. But in the spiritual realm such a mathematical demonstration is not possible. Hence the shortsighted rationalists simply deny the very existence of the divine as well as the demonic.

We will point out how these extrasensory forces reveal themselves by means of a few examples.

Ex. 48. The two Seiler brothers in Ottenheim, Baden, run a non-professional medical practice. One of the brothers puts himself into a trance and in this state he is able to identify the diseases of the patients. The process is always successful.

Ex. 49. In Alsace a Catholic priest heals by magic. His nickname is Father Slipper. The reason behind this is that all those who desire his help must send him one of their slippers. Through concentrating on the slippers he can discover what is wrong with the people.

Ex. 50. During counselling sessions in Austria I happened to come across a so-called urine taster. The patient's urine was not examined medically to discover the albumen, sugar and haemoglobin content etc., but was used as a psychometrical means of contact for a clairvoyant diagnosis. Such urine tasters are also known in Switzerland, France, Germany and other European countries.

The strange thing is that in spite of such curious methods the diagnosis often proves to be correct. These magic healing methods depend on mediumistic and extrasensory forces! Herein lies the reason for their success.

In the definition the various aims of magic were mentioned. Whereas spiritism seeks to communicate with and to dominate the spirit world, magic enlarges this aim to cover people, animals, plants and the material world. The black magician endeavours to subjugate and to dominate his enemy through magic. Some examples of this will follow later. Others try through magic to influence the animal and the plant worlds as we see in the next examples.

Ex. 51. A man dabbled in black magic for many years. He specialized in stealing milk from the neighbouring farmers. He would tie a towel to a door knob, then murmur his magic phrases and squeeze the milk out of the towel. I have heard of similar examples in my counselling work but I was unable to investigate them personally.

Ex. 52. A missionary told me that on several occasions

when she had tried to visit a magician some wild animals had approached her. She felt at once that demonic powers were at work. She had commanded the animals to go in the name of Jesus. They had gone. After this she heard that the magician had boasted that he was able to send out wild animals to kill any foreigner who came to see him.

Ex. 53. A young man, whom a doctor described as schizophrenic, confessed to me during counselling that he had the ability to kill small animals at some distance away from him, merely through using his powers of magic.

Ex. 54. In Toggenburg, Switzerland, on several occasions in my counselling sessions people confessed that they had the power to kill horses, cows and pigs with the help of black magic. In reply to my question how they had received this ability, they told me that they had subscribed themselves with their own blood to the devil. One actual case of animal killing was examined by some scientists but they could find no natural cause of death.

Ex. 55. A farmer who had had several bad crops in a row was given the following advice by a magician. He should place three grains of corn under his tongue while sowing, then, having sowed the field he should spit the corn out of his mouth into the field, say a magic charm and end by calling on the names of the Father, Son and Holy Ghost. This would then encourage growth and protect the crops from bad weather. As a matter of fact the farmer was convinced that the charming of his field had been beneficial. Since that time though, his desire to read the Word of God disappeared, and besides this there was an enormous increase in accidents in his stables.

It is not only the organic world, the world of living creatures, that falls within the sphere and influence of magic, but also the inorganic world of dead matter. The following are some examples of this.

Ex. 56. For years three sisters slept in a single room.

From time to time stones would fall from the ceiling of this room. When the eldest sister became engaged and finally left the house, this rain of stones stopped. I heard of the incident from one of the sisters. Such magical falls of stones are not so rare as one might imagine. I have on several occasions had eyewitness accounts of them.

Ex. 57. For many years a man practised black magic. One of his specialities which he often demonstrated was thrusting a knife into the ground. He would murmur some magical words and several pints of blood would then come out of the place where the knife had been stuck in. The sister of this man was also an expert in the same field. The question is, was this just a clever trick or a genuine piece of magic? This case is very reminiscent of a fakir trick. Nevertheless similar incidents have been reported to me in my pastoral work.

In the sphere of magic some of the most unreasonable things take place. Yet even if it were simply all a case of superstition and imagination, and if it had no real foundation, the area would still be an abyss of human aberration and need, demanding enlightenment and counselling help. Other questions arising from the definition will come under discussion later.

(II) The Origin, Aim and Development of Magic

At the very threshold of human history stands God's command, "Fill the earth and subdue it" (Gen. 1:28). The task and right of man was the peaceful conquest of the earth's powers in accordance with the will of God. In opposition to this command Satan, the great master of confusion came and put forward his arch-temptation, "You will be like God knowing good and evil" (Gen. 3:5). Magic is the very antithesis of the commandment of God as it reveals a hunger for knowledge and a desire for power in opposition to the will of God. When faced with this temptation mankind was at the crossroads.

The decision had to be made. Either voluntary subordination to the will of God or rebellion against His statutes and His ordinances caused by a greed for power and a desire for knowledge. The decision still faces us today. We either conform to God's revealed way of salvation or we carry on the rebellion, trying to rule the created world in unforgivable opposition to God. Magic is thus at its roots a rebellion, and it has been so from the beginning. It is the climax of man's revolt against God. Any talk of harmless forces of nature and neutral applications is criminal in the light of this scriptural fact.

On the surface, parapsychology (the science of extrasensory experiences) still recognizes something of the double nature of magic. The differentiation is made between Psi-Gamma phenomena and Psi-Kappa phenomena. (Gamma representing gignoskein, to perceive; kappa representing kinein, to move). Here we have again the two basic elements of magic: knowledge and power through supernatural means.

Through a great deal of pastoral work I have noticed four ways in which magical powers can originate. These are through heredity, subscription of oneself to the devil, occult experiments and occult transference.

a) The evidence drawn from many actual case histories goes to prove that magical abilities can be passed on by means of heredity. Often mediumistic powers can be traced back over three or four generations in one family. There are two possibilities here, one being that it is a matter of the genes and the other that it is a matter of succession. By this we mean the custom of a person on his deathbed actually bestowing the magical abilities upon the eldest son or daughter in order to die peacefully. Often tragic scenes occur when the children do not want to have these abilities passed on to them. A person may cry out for weeks on his deathbed for someone to relieve him of his magical powers. Sometimes a distant relative or an outsider is willing to accept the succession. The reason for this may differ from case to case, be it pity, curiosity or maybe lust for power. The death of some magicians can drag on over a period of weeks till the office of 'succession' has been settled. This is not an apostolic but a diabolic succession.

b) Magical powers on the other hand may originate through subscription to the devil. One can see in this the counterpart to baptism. To every event recorded in the Bible there seems to be a demonic parallel to it in the field of magic. Subscription to the devil accounts for some of the most terrible and formidable cases met with by Christian workers.

Ex. 58. In Paris there is an occult church with the name or title, 'We Worship the Prince of this World'. This church has sister congregations in Basle and Berne, and just recently one has been opened in Rome. In order to become a member of this church one has to subscribe oneself to the devil. This is a baptism into black magic!

Ex. 59. For years a man in Toggenburg, Switzerland, had a flourishing practice as a nature healer and charmer. He could even cure some people who the doctors had given up as hopeless. He had healed the blind, the lame, cases of advanced cancer, tuberculosis, leukemia, multiple sclerosis, scleroderma and other serious diseases. On one occasion however, the man's own personal need came to the surface. He said, "I can help others, but for myself there is no help, no not in all eternity!" In his youth the man had subscribed himself to the devil. It was since that time that he had obtained his unearthly healing ability.

c) Another way in which magical powers may develop is through experimenting with occultism.

Ex. 60. A Swiss factory worker grew tired of his job.

Since he had often heard that occult healers and mesmerizers made a lot of money he bought some magic literature for himself. He set about learning the magic charms, underwent various devil ceremonies and then began healing experiments. His magic healing ability developed rapidly and ultimately his income surpassed his previous earnings many times over.

The next example will illustrate all three factors together, that is, the factors of heredity, subscription and experimenting in occultism.

Ex. 61. A young woman told me this story. Her great-grandmother had subscribed herself to the devil with her own blood. She had practised black magic and had healed both animals and people. On her deathbed she had suffered terribly as is often the case with magic conjurers. The daughter, that is the grandmother of my storyteller, took over the magic powers of her mother. The magic literature of her mother also passed into her hands. Later the apparition of the great-grandmother was seen by the relatives. The grandmother however, continued to practise magic. During nights of the full moon she would charm diseases. She was also in the habit of using a key suspended over a Bible as a pendulum, and she could also successfully stop people from bleeding. If she ever attempted to read the Bible she found it quite a trial. As she grew older she began to see black figures in her home, and finally when she died it was again an unpleasant time. Her ghost was also seen after her departure. The story went on that the young woman's mother had then taken over the magical literature and practices. She too had become a well-known healer but her fate had been the same as her predecessors'. The fourth member in this terrible line of succession was now the young woman. As a small child her mother had cast spells over her. Shortly after this she had become clairvoyant and had also begun to see black figures in the house. Her brother and sister had suffered from depressions and she herself had had serious psychic and nervous disturbances which had led her to seek the help of a minister.

d) Occult transference is the fourth source of magical powers.

Ex. 62. A young man told me that he had once had three black magicians lay their hands on his head and murmur some magic charms over him. He had afterwards possessed magic abilities which astonished even the family doctor. The doctor had investigated his powers and had to acknowledge that they were genuine. The laying on of the hands of the magicians would again be a counterpart to the scriptural laying on of hands.

Ex. 63. A young man saw someone searching for water with a pendulum. He was asked if he would like to have a go, but the pendulum did not react in his hand. When the dowser took hold of his hands, though, the pendulum had at once reacted. Later when he had tried to repeat the experiment by himself, he was again successful, and he discovered that he now had the ability to search for water with both a rod or a pendulum. Yet the young man felt a change in his Christian life. Previously he had been regular in his reading of the Bible and in prayer. After this transference of pendulum ability, however, his love for the Word of God and for prayer declined.

(III) Forms of Magic

Certain influences, as we might call them, can be termed elementary forms of magic. We will list them.

Firstly we have the criminal use of hypnosis.

Ex. 64. A girl reported in a counselling session that a doctor whom she had consulted had hypnotized her. While hypnotized he had seduced her. The doctor had done the same to her girl friend. It was later discovered that he had also done this with other girls. When these stories leaked out, the doctor left the town and settled elsewhere. The girl said that for a long time after this incident she had not been able to read her Bible. She had felt a strong aversion towards religion, and evil thoughts had always come to her mind when praying.

Ex. 65. A doctor at a hospital had indecently assaulted women and girls under hypnosis. Once the ward sister caught him in the act. To cover up his scandalous behaviour, he used to question the patients about their sexual relationships and included their answers in their case histories. He thus tried to protect himself in the event of anything being discovered. A respectable girl who was engaged to a Christian young man became pregnant at the hospital. Following this her fiancé left her. The girl herself denied all knowledge of having sexual relationships with anyone. The doctor had lain with her when she had been hypnotized. The assistant matron and the ward sister had finally reported the doctor. However, the result was that they themselves were dismissed by the medical superintendent. The doctor in question stayed. Other nurses, who also had incriminating evidence against him, were forced to keep quiet now because of the fear of dismissal. After a few years, though, when the situation became too hot for the doctor, he left and went abroad.

Scientific advocates of hypnosis believe that a man cannot be forced to do anything under hypnosis that he would not be prepared to do when conscious. They are of the opinion that crimes are not possible under hypnosis. But not all the experts share this opinion. Moreover, in my counselling work I have met many cases in which crimes have taken place under hypnosis. From the point of view of the Scriptures it is understandable that an innocent girl can be molested in this way. Jesus said that out of the heart come evil thoughts and so on. Evil lies dormant even in the most moral of people. Normally these instinctive reactions are held in check by one's consciousness, which is moulded by education, religious training and is affected by one's disposition. Under hypnosis however, this regulator is switched off. Instinctive impulses can arise unhindered from the subconscious, and can be exploited by unscrupulous and uninhibited people. Besides this, some take no account of the fact that magical hypnosis exists in addition to the normal type of hypnosis, and that this can have far deeper effects. Magical hypnosis can often be recognized by the fact that afterwards the patient is no longer able to pray or to keep his faith. Here are some actual examples of magical hypnosis.

Ex. 66. A Christian girl went to a psychiatrist. The psychiatrist used magical hypnosis far more often than he did ordinary hypnosis. I have occasionally come across such doctors in areas where magic is commonly practised. In reply to the girl's question, the doctor admitted that he had not received his gift from God. He went on to tell the girl that he had wanted to conduct suggestive experiments on her. After the treatment the girl lost her faith and could no longer pray. She suffered from doubts and other serious difficulties in believing.

Ex. 67. In his spare time a minister dabbled in magic. He experimented in various areas and learned card-laying, how to use a pendulum, magic charming and magic hypnosis. Since he had no suitable people to experiment on, he used his wife for the purpose. As his magical abilities increased, so too did his own and his wife's dislike for the Bible and prayer. This dislike developed into a strong resistance, and as time went on psychic disturbances appeared in the wife. She exhibited a serious anxiety hysteria and always had to lock the door of whichever room she happened to be in.

Ex. 68. A businessman has the strange ability of being able to influence his customers hypnotically or magically, causing them to accept the business offers that he makes to them. In this way his yearly income exceeds £6,000. He rejects Christianity altogether.

Ex. 69. A woman allowed a masseur to hypnotize her. Before the treatment she had regularly read her Bible, prayed and attended the local church services. Afterwards when she tried to pray she felt a compulsion to blaspheme and to curse. She then lost her faith. These effects indicate that the masseur had used magical hypnosis.

In general our doctors understand nothing of magically based hypnosis because it is an occult practice. While normal hypnosis as practised by the medical world may be harmless, hypnosis used in conjunction with magic is always dangerous, and is a burden to the patient concerned.

A second elementary form of magic may be found in the area of mental suggestion. We mean by this a transmission of mental or emotional forces over a distance.

Ex. 70. A young psychologist wanted to qualify as a university lecturer. He specialized in hypnosis, though it was not the normal type of hypnosis but rather mental suggestion. He looked for a sensitive subject for his experiments and found one in the secretary of his boss. She was of nervous debility and easily influenced. Without asking, he attempted to put her to sleep. He would sit down about three or four yards away, either in the same room or a neighbouring one, and then concentrate on her. She would find that her arms would suddenly become limp. A tremendous tiredness would come over her. She would have to fight with all her strength to avoid falling asleep. These experiments were continued over a period of time with the girl always resisting them. During this time the girl gradually developed psychic disturbances. She consulted a psychiatrist. When he heard of the suggestive experiments, he told her that they would not do her any good, as he already knew about the experiments of the young psychologist. The girl, having been the subject of these experiments for a considerable period of time, has since experienced strange paralytic symptoms and is now only capable of doing part-time work.

Ex. 71. A Catholic woman regularly went to confession. As time went on she gradually became psychically and suggestively dependent on the priest. Every time he said the mass she would fall to the ground and injure herself, and it was always her face. This happened even when she was 20 miles away and she could be quite oblivious to the fact he was taking a service. The strange dependence became an unbearable burden to the woman. In her distress she began to pray earnestly, and she went to a Protestant minister for counselling. Through faith she found Christ as a personal Saviour. The attacks immediately vanished. The woman then left the Catholic church.

Ex. 72. For several years a craftsman indulged in black magic. He was chiefly concerned with the influencing of other people through his magic, and he also belonged to a magic circle which itself conducted unusual experiments. His first victim was a sensitive girl. He brought her under his control to such an extent that she sacrificed both her money and her body to him. After this initial success he looked for other victims. He continued to be successful with his experiments, and he finally found a girl who regularly handed over her monthly pay-cheque to him. For this reason he lived with her until finally her parents reported the matter to the police.

A third elementary form of magic is magically based magnetism or mesmerism. Magnetism, together with hypnosis and suggestion, can be magically intensified. Ex. 69 refers to this fact.

For our first examples of this we will turn to Dr.Trampler, a lawyer who was originally a student of Groening, but who later ceased to hold the same ideas. Dr. Trampler has outlined his methods of healing in a book 'Gesundung durch den Geist' (Healing through the Spirit). His most fanatical followers are women. I have seen in counselling people that his healing powers are not beneficial, but are instead a burden to those treated. Two examples can be quoted to indicate this.

Ex. 73. A woman visited Dr. Trampler in Munich. He was successful in treating her backaches. In the course of the treatment he had made her hold her fingers up in the air as if they were antennae for cosmic powers, so he said. On returning home she found that organically she had been healed, but since then her spiritual life was held in check. She, like so many others, now found it impossible to pray and felt as though there was an impenetrable wall between herself and God.

Ex. 74. A Christian woman who came to me for counselling had visited Dr. Trampler in ignorance. While sitting in his office she had prayed. Finally when the other patients had been treated and it was her turn, Dr. Trampler came over to her. She had felt a strange fear come upon her and had prayed all the more. The doctor had then said to her, "I can't do anything for you".

Since these healers often camouflage and garnish their activities with religious phrases, the terrible nature of their powers is often unrecognized. In Baden I gained the acquaintance of a man who had been an unqualified medical doctor. In answer to my question regarding his healing ability he answered, "Natural healing magnetism can enable you to heal about two patients daily. The power is by then used up and one has to be recharged or refilled. People who treat more than two patients a day are either fakes, or they are plugged into the devil." By this he meant that such people would actually be using magic in their practice. Here is one other example of this both frequent yet confusing camouflage.

Ex. 75. A friend of mine, a Christian teacher, was being treated by a mesmerizer who was himself supposed to be a Christian. At least he attended a church. To make sure, the teacher asked the mesmerizer, "You don't use demonic forces, do you?" The man replied, "Why not? Demonic powers are good. Demons are here to help us." The teacher decided not to continue with the treatment!

Having outlined these elementary aspects of magic, we will now go on to the more basic and principal forms. Professor Diepgen in his book 'Culture and Medicine' differentiates between three main forms of magic: black magic which uses demonic forces, white magic which is allegedly promoted by the power of God, and neutral magic which is supposed to rely solely on ordinary forces of nature. Diepgen is correct in dividing magic into three forms, but the same cannot be said of his definitions. Christian pastoral work reveals a completely different picture to the one he suggests concerning neutral and white magic.

a) First however, some examples of black magic.

Ex. 76. A minister informed me that the whole of his congregation had been infected by occultism. As an example he told me of the healing of a 20 year old girl through magic. Because of an attack of polio the girl had had a leg shortened. She had been in the hospital for a long time and then been released as incurable. The girl and her mother were very depressed. In this state they had finally sought the help of a man who practised black magic. This man sold them a mandrake root — for about £45! The root, which in some ways resembled a human figure, according to his directions had to be nursed by the girl as if it were a child. She had to wash it, feed it and put it to bed as if it were really alive. The magician then told the girl to pray and repeat vindictive psalms or songs, and to write them out and sleep with them under her pillow. Next he went on to tell her to stick two knives into the wall above her bed and to put two more knives under the pillow. In spite of this strange treatment the girl discovered that her leg began to grow longer. Finally she was healed, but afterwards she developed serious psychic disturbances. She then went to her minister, but he could give her no advice. The girl could no longer pray. When she tried to clasp her hands together they were torn apart. On attempting to read the Bible she was assaulted with blasphemous thoughts. Fearing the loss of her own sanity the girl gave both the mandrake root and an amulet which she had also received to the minister. Now she lived in the fear that the magician would revenge himself, and her leg, though it had been healed, returned again to its former state.

Ex. 77. During a mission in Toggenburg a farmer came and told me of some unhappy results of black magic charming. His boy had contracted polio. The doctor was called in too late and the boy remained paralysed. Since the farmer had wanted his son to be healthy no matter what the cost, he tried everything. Finally he went to the notorious magician Hugentobler in Peterzell. This man healed the boy with the help of black magic and his paralysis disappeared completely. For several years everything went well, but when the son was 16 years old the father found him in the stable dying from a cut carotid artery. This happened quite out of the blue. The boy had previously shown no signs of unhappiness. On his son, however, the father found an amulet from Hugentobler. Opening the leather pouch he took out a small piece of paper with the inscription, "This soul belongs to the devil". This was proof enough that Hugentobler had used black magic on the boy.

b) White magic is even more wide-spread than black magic. Many Christian groups practise this form of magic oblivious to its demonic character. White magic is a fulfilment of the words of Paul in 2 Cor. 11:14, that even

Satan disguises himself as an angel of light. White magic is black magic under a religious disguise. Here are a few examples.

Ex. 78. A missionary to the Jews in North Africa by the name of Samuels, reported one of their magic customs. When one of their children is ill they take a towel, tie a knot in it and say, "In the name of the God of Abraham, Isaac and Jacob, be released from your sickness". They then untie the knot and the child gets well. This piece of magic charming is a counterpart to black magic.

Ex. 79. A woman from Bukowina told us that her relatives could heal any type of disease in both animals and human beings merely through using white magic charms. By adding the words "In the name of the Father, Son and Holy Ghost" to the spell the sickness would disappear. In spite of a family tradition of church-going, the various spells and charms had been handed down in the family for several generations. Both the woman and her daughter suffer from nervous disturbances. It was for this reason that she had sought the counsel of a minister. Her condition improved after the minister had prayed with her and later she became a convinced Christian.

Ex. 80. The owner of a certain farm hanged himself in his house. According to the popular belief of the villagers the man continued to haunt the place of his death. The relatives were advised to sweep out the whole house repeating the words, "In the name of the Father, Son and Holy Ghost". After this the man's ghost would no longer trouble them. The relatives followed this unusual advice, but afterwards the farmer's wife was troubled by a strange feeling of unrest.

Ex. 81. A fifteen-year-old girl had a disease of the eyes. She spent quite a time in an eye clinic, but in spite of the treatment she was not cured. Since medical help had failed, she turned to a magic charmer. This man, using white magic, made some spells over her. The man actually attended church occasionally and he also kept a Bible in his consulting room. Within 24 hours of the charming, the girl's eye trouble disappeared, but thereafter she felt a terrible inner unrest. She prayed but found no peace. Later, when she visited her former eye specialist, he could only shake his head in astonishment and ask her how she had been healed.

Ex. 82. A woman had her two daughters magically charmed when they were children. During this magical treatment the charmer used the Lord's prayer three times. As the children grew up the mother often resorted to astrology, card-laying and palmistry. On top of all this she also received a monthly magazine from a doctor who practised occultism. Later at the age of 27 the eldest daughter was put into a mental institution. She is thought to be incurable. The whole family was very antagonistic towards religion, but nevertheless they were finally driven, through their psychic distress, to seek the counsel of a Christian minister.

Ex. 83. Another woman, a Christian, had several recipes involving white magic. For example, to cure stomatitis one had to drink some holy water while reciting the names of the Father, Son and Holy Ghost.

Ex. 84. A woman was seriously ill in hospital suffering from shingles and ulcers on her legs. Her condition was so bad that the doctor ordered a nurse to be at her side continually during the night. The nurse was sitting next to the bed of the woman when she began to whisper over and over again, "You can help me, nurse, you can help me, nurse". The nurse was afraid that the woman might want her to pray or to read something from the Bible. But the patient wanted neither. The nurse was so full of fear in the presence of the woman, that she could not have prayed even if she had wanted to. However, the woman continued, "You can help me, nurse, you can help me, nurse". In the end the nurse asked, "How can I help you?" With that the woman became quite excited and explained, "I want you to put your hands on the places on my body which are diseased. Then I want you to make three crosses over them, and to mention the names of the Trinity together with a little verse that I will tell you." By now the nurse was even more frightened. At that moment a doctor came down the corridor. She called to him und asked him if she should do what the woman had asked her. He replied, "You might as well. Humanly speaking there is not much hope for her, and you never know, it might help." The nurse went back to the woman, who again immediately urged her to start the charming process. At last she complied with the patient's wishes, making the crosses and saying what she had been asked to say. When she had finished, the woman at once relaxed and was at rest. However, an even greater fear gripped the nurse. Over the next few days the woman's condition improved beyond all expectation and the doctors were astonished. The ulcers healed up immediately as did all the symptoms of the skin disease. Within five days she was completely well. The doctors could give no reason for her recovery, and the one who had encouraged the nurse to carry on with the charming kept the incident to himself. For the following six years though, the nurse had no rest. She could not pray and she was nauseated by the Scriptures. She suffered from dizziness and could not concentrate, besides having other psychic disturbances. In the end, because of her condition, she came to me for counselling. She traced everything back to the terrible incident in the hospital with the woman. Without realizing it she had participated in some white magic.

In all the above examples of white magic, various Christian symbols play a part in conjunction with the number three. In some cases the names of the Trinity may be used, in others three Lord's prayers, or three crosses or three Bible verses, or even three candles may be used. White magic is a subtle perversion of the scriptural idea of the prayer of faith and the laying on of hands. It is because of the subtlety that so many fall victim to this religious form of magic.

To distinguish between white magic and true laying on of hands is often quite difficult, even when the basic differences are known. In the true prayer of faith, the person concerned submits completely to the will of God. In white magic the idea is to compel God to act. With true prayer God is really involved, whereas in white magic the name of God is only used by way of a technical formula. Genuine prayer is inspired by the Holy Spirit. The white magician is inspired by the powers of darkness. Those who pray as the Scriptures direct are strengthened in their faith, even when their prayers are apparently unanswered. Those involved in white magic invariably have their faith paralysed, that is if they had any previously. However, through white magic some may even obtain what they actually desired, and so it is often only in the effects that its true nature is revealed. The boundary between prayer and magic can be very fluid. Sometimes it is essential to have the gift of discerning of spirits if one is to be able to differentiate between the genuine and the imitation articles. Another difference is that white magic requires no counselling procedure before it can be applied, whereas in the case of the laying on of hands and prayer this is an absolute necessity, even if it is only between the person concerned and God Himself. White magic either hinders prayer or makes it impossible. Laying on of hands, as the apostles did, strengthens prayer. So then we see that white magic and prayer with the laying on of hands are at entirely opposite poles, even though white magic may sometimes draw upon certain words and phrases from the Scriptures.

c) Yet another form of magic is the so-called neutral

magic. It has recently been introduced into the practice of doctors of the psychomatic school. Some believe that one can use neutral forces of nature for healing purposes. I have several examples in front of me but they are difficult to classify.

Ex. 85. A young doctor who had a lot of warts on his hand asked the leader of a psychosomatic seminar, "Professor, how is it possible to get rid of warts?" The professor replied that the only sure way was to use charming. The doctor took his advice and discovered that the magic charming was a complete success. I have heard nothing of the after effects in this case, so I can make no comment in this direction.

Ex. 86. A young psychiatrist asked the principal of a psychiatric clinic the same question. He was given the following advice. "Wind a black thread around the warts and tie as many knots in the thread as you have warts. Then repeat a magic spell while placing the thread under a piece of guttering. That's how you can get rid of the unsightly things." The psychiatrist at first thought it was a joke, but he was finally talked into trying it out. The experiment turned out to be a success. The warts in fact disappeared.

The advice in this particular case was not neutral magic. This strange recipe is to be found in the 6th and 7th Book of Moses which contains only black or white magic charms. Until now this supposedly neutral form of magic has not proved its own neutrality. My counselling work continually supplies evidence to the effect that magic in any form is the work of the devil, whether it sails under a black, white or neutral flag.

(IV) Areas of Applied Magic

In the section dealing with the aims of magic, we have already mentioned that everything in the created universe can come under its fire. Magic plays a part in Satan's world-wide rebellion against God and Christ. Through it he attacks angels and spirits, animals and men and everything in the material world. It is simply impossible to describe the tremendous scope of magic in a single book. We will, though, mention the main areas in which magic comes into play.

First, healing and the inflicting of diseases. A number of examples on healing have already been given so we will only add one more.

Ex. 87. A Catholic woman was seriously ill in hospital. The woman called the nurse and asked a favour of her. She went on to say that she had a daughter at home who had been demon-possessed for many years, and that the daughter was rarely conscious. Being so seriously ill the woman now saw an opportunity of helping her daughter. She asked the nurse to get in touch with her relatives before she died. She wanted the relatives to bring the daughter to the hospital so that the two of them could change vests with one another. Her idea was that in doing so her daughter would be freed, while she would die in the state of being possessed. The nurse however, did not fulfil her wish.

Inflicting diseases is directly opposite to healing.

Ex. 88. A young man wanted to evade military service. His father therefore sent him to a magic charmer to be given some illness. The experiment was successful, and afterwards the young man was found to be unfit for military service.

Ex. 89. A spiritistic medium confessed that she belonged

to a circle which not only practised communication with the dead but also black magic. Her speciality was in causing sicknesses and in death magic; she had already committed several murders which the police had been unable to solve. She had also worked on a minister who afterwards developed nervous disturbances and had been unable to work for several months. This was the content of her confession. I could not prove the statements, but I did know that at the time of the circle's magic experiments this particular minister had been ill for a considerable period of time.

Ex. 90. A girl from a strict Catholic family married a Protestant against the will of her parents. The first child they had contracted polio. The parents blamed their daughter, saying that it was her punishment for marrying a Protestant. Later they asked a magician to heal the baby boy and to transfer the illness to the mother instead. This in fact happened and the child was cured, while the girl herself became ill. She was taken to a hospital with symptoms of paralysis, depressions and terrible headaches. The doctors differed in their diagnosis. They made one test after another; spinal puncture, metabolism test, electro-cardiogram etc. Finally they called in a brain specialist. She was examined over a period of several weeks but no cause was found for her illness. Later the condition of the young woman improved rapidly and she asked to be discharged. She was allowed to go home. Her parents, on hearing about this, were greatly disturbed and immediately reported the matter to the magician, telling him that his persecution of her had become ineffective.

Ex. 91. A black magician told a girl who was being courted by a married man, "I'll break this man's mind so much that he'll lose his position." It was not very long after this that the man began to have nervous disorders. He would complain of hearing noises both in his head and externally. He also suffered from flickering before the eyes, loss of vision and an inability to concentrate.

Ex. 92. A girl became a Christian during a mission. Inspired by the joy of her salvation she invited others to the meetings. It so happened that nearby there lived a man who possessed an extensive amount of occult literature and who practised its contents. The girl's joy, coupled with her witnessing, got on his nerves. (The gospel of Christ and magic are as far apart as heaven and hell). The occultist threatened to drive her mad and to prevent her from going to the mission. Within weeks the girl began suffering from various disturbances. She would sometimes see small flames of light in her room together with other ghostly phenomena. It was then that she had come to me for counselling.

Secondly, love and hate magic. Examples 90, 91 and 92 could be included under the heading of hate magic and so we will only add a couple of examples on love magic.

Ex. 93. The Swiss herdsmen who bring the cattle down from the summer pastures in September like to tie three different herbs into the rope of the leading cow. This serves not only as a means of decoration but is also meant to bring luck in love.

Ex. 94. A girl had an affair with a married man. The man later moved away from the district, but before he left he said to the girl, "Though we will be separated now, I will continue to visit you. I won't drive back here, but I will visit you in your dreams. You know what a man wants from a girl, and I will be able to take what I need any time I like. You won't be able to prevent it, and you will never be able to take any action against me as there will be no evidence to support your story." At first the girl did not understand what her lover had really meant, but a week after her friend had left she suddenly felt his presence during the night. These visits were repeated again and again until they became a terrible and disgusting experience to the girl. First she consulted a doctor, but as was to be expected the doctor explained the nightly psychic meetings away by saying that they were sexual hallucinations related to the first stages of schizophrenia. The girl could not accept this diagnosis, as she was mentally quite normal. She was convinced that it was more than an hallucination.

Thirdly, persecution and defence magic. These are among the most common forms of magic.

Ex. 95. Two Boldavian women who had practised magic for many years were involved in a quarrel. They each used their magical powers to attack the other. One of the women fell to the ground, apparently without cause. She seemed to be paralysed and could not get up again. She swore and cursed at her opponent. As she was being lifted up from the ground she screamed at the other woman, "You won't leave this house alive — I'll see to that." Three days later the second woman had a terrible headache and within just over a week she died.

Ex. 96. A child used to cry every night from 11 to 1 o'clock. The mother was desperate and took the advice of a magician. She was told to put a knife, a fork and a pair of scissors under the child's pillow in order to stop the trouble. She was also told that the person who was causing the child's unrest would, because of the defence magic, injure himself. The mother, as we have said, followed this advice. The next day the maid had a bandage on, and the mother was convinced that she had been the cause of the nightly disturbances.

Ex. 97. A farmer discovered that the milk of one of his cows had blood in it. He took the milk and just before midnight he heated it up. At the same time he thrust a sickle into it murmuring a magic spell. The next day a woman who lived nearby had some facial injuries, and the farmer was thereby convinced that this woman had bewitched his cow.

Fourthly, casting and breaking spells. This is practised by some magicians as if it were a sport, while others use it to further their own interests.

Ex. 98. A man in a Christian convalescent home had the power to cast and to break magic spells. He could stop a person in the street in such a way that he would neither be able to move nor speak. He could also put a ban on children so that they too would be both speechless and unable to move. This man was supposed to be a Christian!

Ex. 99. In Switzerland an officially licensed mesmerizer treats his patients by using white magic charms. He uses either three Lord's prayers or the names of the Trinity. Because of these religious phrases his patients believe him to be a Christian. However, when a patient does not pay him at once he puts them under a spell so that they are not able to board a train when they get to the station. The ticket collector and others at the station are so familiar with the magic powers of the mesmerizer that by now they laugh it off and merely tell the patient that he must first go back and pay the man if he wants to be able to get on a train.

Ex. 100. For many years a school teacher indulged in black magic. He not only provided himself with literature on the subject, but also experimented with the magic. He used his school children as guinea pigs. He would ask a child a question and at the same time put the boy or girl under a spell. They would then neither be able to stand up nor utter a word. Only after he had lifted the ban would the child be able to answer his question. He used a similar method to punish the children. After practising this for some time on his school children, he started making his own wife and daughter the subjects of further experiments. He ruled his family so completely that he could cast spells over them at will. Sometimes they were unable to say a word for hours or even days at a time. His wife was psychically destroyed in the end, and she died. His second wife soon left him and never returned after his first banning experiment. The man then turned to sexual attacks on his daughter. She was completely powerless to defend herself. Later, when her father turned his attentions towards a third woman, he put a spell on the daughter so that she suffered a permanent paralysis of speech. Finally because his daughter came between himself and his many women friends he had her committed to a mental institution. The doctors were unable to cure the paralysis in her speech, and her relatives, though conscious of the terrible home background, were forbidden by the father to visit the unfortunate girl in the hospital.

Lastly, death magic. Here we come to one of the darkest areas that exists in magic. I have reports of this from several missionaries in front of me. Very few people realize that this type of magic is still being practised in Europe today. Even if its effectiveness cannot be proved, its mere existence implies that our culture is still at a very low level.

Ex. 101. An expert in black magic specialized in magic persecution and death magic. With the help of his magic he was able to kill a cow within four days. This story was verified by the man's grandson.

Ex. 102. For many years a woman practised black magic. She possessed some very dangerous magic books; for instance the 6th and 7th Book of Moses, the Spring Book, the Spiritual Shield, and many others. She experimented in the area of magic persecution and death magic and she even boasted of having caused the deaths of her husband and daughter. She would inflict her enemies with diseases and claimed that she was able to cause eczemas, diarrhoea, heart trouble, itching, stomach pains, swelling of the body and other things. After causing the death of all the members of her family, according to her own words, she then took on the job of a district nurse.

She obtained this job with the help of the local minister, but the woman still practises her magic arts. Her mind is completely opposed to the things of God and she calls Jesus an illegitimate good-for-nothing. At Christmas and Easter and other such times she suffers from terrible attacks, during which she will rage and blaspheme. On other occasions, however, her conscience bothers her and she will admit that her life is in a mess. "I don't want to do these things, but I am forced to. The devil makes me do them. I can't rest or relax any more." This is her testimony!

Ex. 103. A married man carried on an adulterous relationship with an older woman. The woman was reputed to indulge in black magic. One day the man tired of his illicit affair. He told the woman that he wanted to break off his relationship with her. She was very upset and threatened him, saying that if he did so then his wife and two children would suffer in the process. The man however, was determined to break it off and stuck to his decision. Two days later his son became ill. They rushed him to the hospital but he died there. The doctors were unable to diagnose the disease. Later still his wife and daughter also fell ill. The man was by now quite frightened and remembered the threats of the woman with whom he had had the affair. He went to her and begged her not to use black magic against his family. She softened and said that she would stop. Thereupon his wife and daughter recovered quickly.

Ex. 104. During a mission a man came to be counselled and reported the following case from his village. One of his neighbours, a farmer, had his new saw stolen. The theft took place in broad daylight and the thief was known to the villagers. The farmer was immediately notified and told who had stolen the saw. He was not content to merely inform the police though. Instead, the farmer went to a man who carried out experiments in persecution through the use of black magic. He payed a considerable amount of money to the occultist, who promised his immediate help, stating that the thief would die. The farmer then drove back to his village and within three hours of his interview with the occultist the thief had a fatal heart attack.

(V) Magic Rites

Almost everything about magic, including the forms it takes and the customs associated with it, gives one the impression that it is a religion of the devil. It everywhere seeks to mimic the world of faith as we find it revealed in the Bible.

There is a liturgy associated with magic which is a counterpart to the true method of worship as revealed in the Scriptures. As an act of worship is composed of certain elements, so too is an act of magic. There are basically four constituents that are necessary. Invoking, charming, a symbolic action, and the use of a fetish. One may invoke either Satan or even the Trinity, and it is this that decides whether the magic is to be black or white. Such invoking is a counterpart to our addressing of God in prayer, as for example, when we say 'Our Father'. The charm or spell that then follows brings the force of magic into play. This imitates our use of the Scriptures and our reference to the promises of the Bible. The symbolic action underlines and supports the charm and mimics such scriptural actions as, for instance, the laying on of hands or kneeling in prayer. The use of a fetish, that is a magically charged object, corresponds perhaps to the use of water in baptism or bread and wine in the case of the Lord's supper.

Ex. 105. A farmer's son suffered repeatedly from a severe pain in his knee. He took the advice of a magic charmer and carried out the following procedure. On a night when the moon was on the wane he went out into a field. He then invoked the Trinity, repeated a magic charm, anointed his knee with oil and finally threw kisses at the moon. Afterwards the pains left him!

This example clearly illustrates what we have just said. The invoking of the Trinity reveals that white magic was used. The magic charm replaced a prayer. Anointing with oil was the symbolic action and the moon acted as the fetish. As the moon waned so the pain left him.

Magic symbolism is supposed to enhance the effectiveness of the charm. A certain amount of magic transference is also involved here. Because of lack of space we cannot discuss the matter at any length so I will only quote a few examples to shed a little light on the subject.

Ex. 106. Professor Frobenius, the well-known spelaeologist (cave researcher), reported in a lecture that some of the cave drawings of stone-age man could be understood as hunting magic. The animals had been drawn as if wounded. This would tally with the hunting magic that is still used today by primitive tribespeople in Africa. It has been reported that native tribes in Africa using this type of magic are actually successful. They draw the animals they wish to kill and then shoot at the pictures while repeating some magic spells. Later the same day they come across animals with the same wounds as those previously drawn. This primitive hunting magic corresponds with similar observations made in Germany. When the apparition of a man or animal is injured, then the medium responsible for the phantom suffers in the same way.

Ex. 107. To cure toothache the following method of charming is prescribed. A new nail must be pushed into the gums three times. It must then be buried in a cellar facing East. A magic charm must be repeated while doing this.

Ex. 108. A school child had a swelling on one arm. The following charm was made. An egg was buried with a stone on top of it while a charm was repeated. As the egg disintegrated in the soil so the swelling was supposed to go down. It did!

Magic symbolism as we have said is usually supported by the use of a fetish. These magically charged objects are supposed to convey the power of the magic. A fetish may consist of some human bones, a bat, urine or excrement, some pubic hair, finger nails, wood from a coffin or anything like this. Any object that has been magically charmed and thereby magically charged may be used as a fetish. Some examples:

Ex. 109. A minister's wife was given a salve by a woman in the church. The salve had been produced by a magic charmer and he had cast spells over it. The salve brought rapid relief. It acted as a fetish rather than a medicine. After this treatment however, the wife of the minister broke her arm. Her daughter also, whose Christian life had until then been continually growing, now found faith and prayer impossible.

Ex. 110. I was told during a mission in Switzerland that a certain Catholic monastery gives little amulets or fetishes to the people to protect them against diseases and epidemics. They consist of small bags, and one in particular contained some toe nails and some egg shell. This may sound improbable, but I am sad to say that I have often witnessed the fact that certain monasteries even practise magic.

There is much debate about the significance of magic words and phrases. Traugott Egloff of Zurich, a well-known representative of charming, speaks of the direct relationship between the words of a charm and the power that produces the miracle. He goes so far as to say that the words themselves are the power. We would say, though, that when a charmer uses biblical phrases, in doing so he severs them from God and deifies the words in their isolation. This isolation leads to a mere mechanical usage, and hence empties the words of their true meaning. Professor Bender has aptly said, "The mechanical is the real essence of the magical and the diabolical."

When, however, the words have been isolated and severed from God, they have no real independent existence, and foreign contents flood in. That which is severed and cut off from God falls prey to the devil. The mechanical and magical usage of the words of the Bible is thus demonic and occult in nature. The Word of God given for the salvation of man is thereby employed as a magical technique to burden and to destroy men.

We would oppose the belief that a word has any power of its own, and that the charmer is only the representative of this power. Words are only neutral instruments. They can be used for either good or evil. It depends on the inspiration behind the words. A Christian employs the Word on God's authority. The magician and charmer employs his words and phrases as demonized instruments of magic.

Ex. 111. A minister told me of the way someone in his parish had died. The man in question had the reputation of being a magician. Two weeks before his death, as he lay in bed seriously ill, he began to groan, "Take the charm away from me, take the charm away from me." The relatives had gone to the minister for advice, but he had warned them against doing as the man requested. The magician finally died in terrible agony. The minister told me that the man looked as black as coal when he had seen him in the coffin. Many magicians only find rest when someone takes the spell or charm away from them, together with the responsibility of carrying on the occult practice.

A description of magic ritual can be found in various books on magic. These books have the same significance to the magician as the Bible has for the Christian. There is a great amount of literature on the subject of magic, the most widely distributed book on the subject being the 6th and 7th Book of Moses. Unhappily a publisher in Braunschweig has published new editions of this book. The use of the name Moses is only a camouflage. Magicians look on the miracle connected with the staff of Moses as a piece of magic. In this way they try to elevate Moses to the position of their patron saint. The first part of the book reveals how a man may enter into a relationship with the devil. The latter part gives instructions as to how a person can achieve dominion over all the forces of nature as well as the powers of heaven and hell through the use of magic. The book has already caused untold harm in the world and people who read it invariably suffer in the process. A house in which the book is kept is also a place where misfortunes often occur. There are many examples which illustrate this fact and we will deal with this problem later on in greater detail. For the moment it will be seen that examples 113 and 115 belong to this category.

(VI) The Effects of Magic and How to Overcome Them

The cost of indulging in magic is extremely high. Every example drawn from the counselling work of Christians reveals the terrifying effects.

a) The principle of compensation. At least on the surface of things magic parallels the facts of the Scriptures. Nevertheless in its effects it is diametrically opposed to the Bible. God's help builds up and gives new strength, whereas magic robs and destroys and tears down. The help of magic is only an apparent help. It merely shifts the load to another area. A small relief in one department is paid for by an excessive stress in another. The compensation is far in excess of the help one apparently experiences. Satan cheats his victims every time. Two examples of this:

Ex. 112. During the birth of a baby girl the midwife noticed that the child had a rupture. This was not treated at once but the midwife advised the family to take some of the excrement of the child and to bury it in a place which was out of reach of the light of both the sun and the moon. They took this strange advice and the infant's rupture disappeared. However, as the child grew up she developed a festering of her nasal bone. A purulant discharge constantly drained from her nose. No medical treatment helped. By her late twenties the trouble had still not cleared up, and in addition to this complaint the girl suffered from a compulsion to swear. She often had to scream and curse and she would shake for no apparent reason.

Ex. 113. For many years a man engaged in black magic with the help of the 6th and 7th Book of Moses. He ended up in an asylum. His wife continued to practise black magic and she suffered the same fate. The son then took over his parents' occult literature. He too ended in an asylum. Again his wife carried on the occult tradition. She also became mentally disturbed and had to be confined to an institution. The whole family had thus been destroyed by the book and its contents. Later a neighbour who was a friend of the afflicted family got hold of the book. He was driven by curiosity to try out the black magic charms contained in it. He too fell victim to the same forces and ended up in a mental home.

b) The wrong defence. The question now arises as to how one can face up to black magic. Is there any effective defence? Some people traditionally believe that white magic has a nullifying effect on black magic. But experience proves that this is not the case. The possibility should not even be considered since white magic has the same demonic character as black magic. Satan would be divided against Satan. Occasionally, however, two magicians may use their powers against one another. Here it is a case of the strongest man winning. It is not a matter of them being in different camps. When a wrestler wins the contest it is because of his superior strength or skill. The two contestants are both wrestlers. For an example of such a duel one can refer back to Ex. 95.

c) Our spiritual weapons. The apostle Paul wrote, "The weapons of our warfare are not worldly but have divine power to destroy strongholds" (2 Cor. 10:4). The believer's prayer can destroy the power of magic. It makes no difference whether it is black or white magic. The effect of prayer is the same. A few examples:

Ex. 114. A Christian had a mesmerizer attend his son who was ill. The father prayed that Christ would prevent the healing if the mesmerizer used evil powers. The healer came and looked at the boy and said at once, "I can't help him."

Ex. 115. A man with tuberculosis of the bones had the disease charmed away using white magic. After the charming the pains immediately ceased. The man himself practised various forms of magic. He also kept many books on magic at his house, as for instance The Seven Locks of Heaven, The Blessing of Tobias, The Letter of Protection from John, Chainletters, and Lucky Letters. He even carried letters of protection like these around with him sewn into his clothing. One day, in great anguish of mind, he tried to become a Christian. But he could not pray. He wanted to trust in Christ but at the same time he felt a violent antagonism within himself towards Christ and His Word. In this state he came to be counselled. In the process he handed over his books on magic and afterwards experienced a definite relief and a relaxation of his previous mental condition.

Ex. 116. A woman with church affiliations suffered from

depressions. During one attack she cut her wrists. The neighbours discovered her in time and called for a doctor at once. Only a blood transfusion saved her life. Afterwards the woman visited a friend of mine who advised her to go to see a Christian doctor. Since the doctor lived some distance away she preferred to take the advice of an older woman in the church who told her to go and see a magic charmer. However, this healer, to her surprise, said "I can can't help you as too many people are praying for you. If they stop praying you can come back. Otherwise I cannot help you." My friend heard later about this and confirmed that he and his wife had been praying for the woman for a long time.

Ex. 117. A man arranged a meeting one evening for the purpose of demonstrating some occult experiments. However, the local minister who was a Christian assembled some of the men of his congregation in order to attend the meeting and to pray during the demonstration. They did this and that evening the experiments of the occultist were unsuccessful. The man in the end exclaimed excitedly that there were some counter forces present which were interfering with his powers. He asked the trouble makers to leave, but the believers would not do so since they had payed for their tickets. The lecture in experimental occultism was a flop.

Ex. 118. A Christian couple lived in the house of a woman who engaged in black magic. The woman magician said to them once that she knew how to get rid of people without them being aware of it. She used to carry on magic experiments in which she tried to influence and trouble people whom she took a dislike to. When the Christian family put themselves under the protection of Christ, though, the woman was infuriated because she could no longer trouble or influence them.

Ex. 119. A paralysed engineer was treated by a magic charmer. Two of his sisters who were Christians prayed a great deal for their brother to be healed. The charmer had no success with his treatment and said, "I cannot help you. Someone is praying for you."

These examples indicate that genuine prayer hinders the use of magic. Previously we have seen that people treated magically find it difficult to pray or to have faith, but the reverse is also true. The power of magic can be warded off by the spiritual weapons of our faith.

Deliverance is through Christ. Psychiatrists, psychotherapists, psychologists and the like are not qualified to treat people subjected to magic. Magical subjection is neither a medical nor a psychological problem but one which concerns faith and the Scriptures. Relief and deliverance are only possible through Christ. It is only when the person subjected to occultism desires to come to Christ that a genuine and complete deliverance is possible.

Ex. 120. A woman who was a missionary became acquainted with a girl in a Christian boarding house who in her youth had subscribed herself to the devil. The landlady told the missionary that she could not handle the girl. Later the missionary asked the girl to come to her room, and there the battle commenced. Her counselling and intercession led to the complete deliverance of the possessed girl.

Ex. 121. A young man courted a girl who was socially higher than himself. Normally he would have had little hope of success. To arrive at his goal he subscribed himself to the devil. He cut his finger and wrote a contract in his own blood on a piece of paper which he later left in a cave. In this way he tried to obtain the help of some love magic. After a while, however, he became scared. He went back to the cave but the paper had disappeared. Nevertheless he later proposed to the girl and they were married. She was a very pretty young woman, but when she gave birth to twins, they were both horribly disfigured.

The mother was so distressed that she died soon after giving birth. The man continued to suffer as he had done so ever since his subscription to the devil, and he was finally driven to seek the help of a minister. After confessing everything and renouncing all that he had had to do with the evil powers, he turned his life over to Christ. Following his conversion he became a living witness to Christ, and although a year and a half later he went to be with his Master, he died in peace, a happy man.

Ex. 122. A girl married a man who brought the 6th and 7th Book of Moses into their marriage. The wife began to suffer from a state of anxiety and she started seeing ghosts at night and feeling an unseen power which seemed to try to strangle her. The husband was an evil tempered man who used to beat his wife. When she was expecting a baby he forced her to bring about an abortion with the aid of tablets. He also demanded perverse things of her, until finally, wanting to put an end to it all, she took eight sleeping pills and some ammonia in an attempt to commit suicide. She was saved just in time. Later she came to be counselled and she received assurance of her own salvation.

Ex. 123. For many years a woman lived in the house of a magic charmer. During the nights she was often frightened by strange incidents involving ghosts. A black figure often appeared in her room and sometimes she saw snakes there. In her fear and distress she came for counselling. She put her trust in the Lord Jesus Christ and afterwards each evening she consciously put herself in God's hands. The ghost phenomena disappeared completely.

Ex. 124. The wife of a dean was emotionally disturbed. In addition to this she exhibited various mediumistic abilities. She had visual and acoustic hallucinations. A Christian girl came to take care of this sick woman and at the same time began to pray for her. Gradually the girl got the impression that the patient was not only emotionally disturbed but also occultly subjected. When one day the woman had another attack the girl commanded the evil power to leave in the name of Jesus. Immediately the patient quietened down.

Ex. 125. A Christian woman interceded for another woman suffering from depressions. Afterwards the depressions completely left the second woman and she became a happy and normal person again. However, from then on the woman who had prayed for her had strange experiences at night. She had the feeling that there was somebody in the room who wanted to kill her. Her whole body shook and she was terribly frightened. Finally she prayed and commanded the power of evil in the name of Jesus to depart. The evil force then disappeared and troubled her no longer.

Ex. 126. The well-known Christian, Alfred Zeller, was asked by a woman for some advice. Her child, she said, was plagued each night from 12 to 1 o'clock, and during this time the child would scream terribly. Zeller questioned the woman about her care of the child, whether the baby was properly fed and so on. He did not share the woman's opinion that it was a case of magic persecution. However, because the woman kept coming to see him he finally went to her house and prayed for the child under the laying on of hands. While Zeller was praying the door opened and a dark thick-set man entered the room. Without a greeting he demanded to know what was going on. Zeller looked up at the intruder and was struck by the evil gaze of the stranger. Zeller prayed quietly and stared back at the man. A spiritual duel developed. Neither man averted his eyes. Inwardly Zeller continued to pray, "The Lord is victorious." The stranger's gaze weakened and he turned and hurried out. Christ had overcome. A few weeks later it was reported that the man had drowned himself in a lake.

All these examples show that Christ can completely overcome the effects of magic. "If the Son makes you free you will be free indeed" (Jn. 8:36). "The reason the Son of God appeared was to destroy the works of the devil" (1 Jn. 3:8). "Christ has delivered us from the dominion of darkness" (Col. 1:13). The basic need of a person subjected and burdened by occultism is for him to turn to Christ. Without this act of faith, real deliverance is impossible. At the end of the chapter on Spiritism we will deal with the question of counselling procedure more fully. At the moment it suffices to say that victory belongs to our Lord Jesus Christ. Paul writes of this victory in Col. 2:15. Jesus has disarmed all the principalities and powers of evil. They have been taken prisoner and publicly paraded as such for all the world to see. Our Lord leads the victory procession. He has triumphed!

Chapter Three

Spiritism

Spiritism has become a threat to both the Christian Church and the Christian message. Pastoral work reveals just how many people who call themselves Christians have come under its spell and have been deceived by it. There is an urgent need in evangelism today for enlightenment on this subject. It is this that prompts me to put into writing the experiences that I have had in my counselling work that deal with spiritism.

In almost every town and city one can find spiritistic circles. A professor of the University of Zurich told me that in one town in Switzerland alone there were about 400 spiritistic circles, and that in another town there were more than 200. On top of this it is estimated that there are about 70 million adherents to spiritism in the world. The essence of spiritism has been made clear to me personally through the many counselling sessions that I have had with individuals affected by it, and it is by this means that I have gained an insight into the shocking background of this anti-Christian movement. One finds it possible with several thousand cases at one's disposal to form a decided judgement on the matter. As has already been pointed out, my book 'Christian Counselling and Occultism' goes at length into the scientific side of these issues, and those seeking further knowledge on the subject are recommended to turn to its pages. Concerning the use of the word 'case' in connection with this subject, some have raised valid criticisms about it. In the English language there are only the two words, 'case' and 'example', to choose from. But though I use these words, it must be pointed out that to me no one I counsel is just a 'case' or an 'example'. They are people for whom Christ has died.

The word 'spiritism' comes from the Latin 'spiritus', spirit. The movement of spiritism represents the endeavour to communicate with the dead in the spirit world. Historically, spiritism can also be traced back over thousands of years. We have testimonies concerning it in the Old Testament in 1 Sam. 28 and Deut. 18. It is also evidenced in the history of the Christian Church. Spiritism seems to be strongly connected with religion and religions. The non-Christian religions are to a large extent spiritistically orientated. But if it were only to show itself in those faiths which are apart from the Christian Faith, the Christian worker would not have to investigate the subject very deeply. However, in so-called Christian countries such a variety of spiritistic forms, and such a range of associated psychic troubles exist, that the need for clarification is a pressing issue in evangelistic work. During thirty-five years as an evangelist I have been confronted by about 16 different types of spiritistic practices which can be divided into five main groups. We will by means of examples be looking at these different forms of spiritism, and then to conclude the chapter we will see what the Bible and medicine have to say concerning the problem, and the counselling procedure one should adopt when seeking to help people affected by spiritism.

Basically this chapter is only a brief statement of the facts. Yet it is hoped that through it the reader will gain a greater insight into the matter, and hence the aim is not so much to arrive at the correct theoretical explanation as to shed light on the spiritual conflict one is faced with in Christian counselling.

(I) Psychical Phenomena

In his counselling work the evangelist or Christian worker sometimes finds that a person will suddenly begin to talk about his spiritual experiences, as for example veridical dreams, apparitions or a vision he may have had. This should always serve as a warning to the counsellor, and he should exercise the greatest restraint and caution in such circumstances. There is no doubt that the Holy Spirit does work in a miraculous way even today. However, a genuine experience in this area is always marked by an attitude of deep humility. Those who make a spiritual sensation, or rather an unspiritual sensation, out of such an experience disclose an artificiality, which unfortunately typifies the majority of today's so-called spiritual experiences. One can say that about nine out of ten cases where people claim that they have had some experience of God or the miraculous are not genuine. We live in a world which has turned its back on God. Together with sin, the demonic and the satanic have complete freedom. The overwhelming conviction that is forced upon one is that we are now living in the special era in which the false prophet in Revelation is to be revealed. The words of the apostle Paul are being literally fulfilled before our very eyes, "Satan disguises himself as an angel of light. So it is not strange if his servants also disguise themselves as servants of righteousness" (2 Cor. 11:14—15). In the field of spiritism the truth of this statement and warning is clearly seen.

Ex. 127. A theological student came for counselling and asked if there was any explanation for an experience he had had. He said that on many occasions he had seen Christ in a vision at night. But the appearances had always caused him to have an uneasy feeling of fear rather than joy. I explained to him that it is possible for Christ to appear to people, but that usually a vision of this nature is caused by some other means. Sometimes it is a result of the outer projection of a vivid religious imagination. In the field of psychology it is recognized that an eidetic can see his own inner ideas as optic pictures. As well as this, a vision can be some form of hallucination. We see from the Bible that a genuine vision of Christ produces a feeling of sinfulness in the one blessed by such an experience. This conviction of inner unworthiness is not to be confused with a feeling of fear. The student saw the difference at once and said that he had had no sense of his own sinfulness at the time, but only this feeling of fear. I then asked him whether he or his relatives had ever engaged in occult practices. He admitted that his mother and grandmother were active spiritists, and that they practised glass-moving. The character of these so-called visions of Christ now came to light. They were a mediumistic and not a spiritual phenomenon.

Ex. 128. A certain man was an active spiritist. For years he practised table-lifting and considered this to be a way of communicating with the dead. He continued with his occult practices so intensively that psychic disturbances set in. The effects of his spiritistic interests also appeared in his children and grandchildren. His oldest son committed suicide. His next son suffered from a persecution mania. His oldest daughter ended up in an insane asylum. Another daughter suffered from Parkinson's disease. Among his grandchildren the same picture emerged. One of them was a schizophrenic. Another suffers from weak nerves and hypersensitivity, and yet another lives a dissolute life, and has given birth to an illegitimate child. The first of the man's great-grandchildren is now a psychopath and a delinquent.

From the scientific point of view one might consider these effects to have a different cause from that of spiritism. The psychiatrist will be interested in the question whether the practising of spiritism was rather the effect than the cause of the ensuing mental and emotional disorders. Or again, was there some latent disposition in the family that was merely triggered off by the spiritistic activities? The parapsychologist will explain the table-lifting phenomenon as psychic automatism, that is an activation of subconscious forces. The Christian however is concerned essentially with the frequency in which psychic disturbances appear in connection with the practice of occultism.

Ex. 129. A young woman came for counselling. She complained about various mental disturbances which included being tired of life and having depressions. Added to this she often had violent fits of temper, and her marriage was being undermined by her own frigidity. It had also happened that the husband had seen strange figures in the house at night. He had not at first told his wife about this so as not to upset her, but after a while she too had seen similar strange and maimed figures about the house. I questioned the woman about her past illnesses and about the general health of her parents and grandparents, but she was the only one to have suffered in this way. In answer to my question about contact with occultism, after a lot of thought she told me the following story. As a young girl she had been a member of a Protestant girl's group. The minister's wife, who had been the leader, used to practise table-lifting with all of the girls. The sessions had always begun with the question, "Spirit, are you there?" One knock had meant 'yes', two had meant 'no'. When the spirit had been willing to answer they had all taken part in asking it questions. The minister's wife had continued this practice for many years until she was paralysed by a stroke. The woman told me that all the girls had subsequently been afraid to visit their leader since her face had been changed into a terrible grimace by the stroke.

Medical science would classify this example together

with the previous one, Ex. 128. Yet with regards to the stroke I would like to point out that in my own experience numerous cases of suicides, fatal accidents, strokes and insanity are to be observed among occult practitioners.

Ex. 130. A bailiff told me that his mother-in-law had the gift of prevision. With the aid of glass-moving she could foretell the future. During the war she had once surprised her family with the statement, "Hubert will die in Latvia through death from the air." Hubert was in fact a relative and it so happened that six months later he was killed in an air attack. It can be added that the woman in question always consulted the glass before making any kind of decision.

For the scientist the question of prevision raises quite a problem. In 'Christian Counselling and Occultism' I have listed the thirty most well-known theories on clairvoyance. Occasionally other theories turn up in the literature of modern parapsychology. Some speak of a magical astral world-soul. This entails the idea of an inner world in which all the occurrences of the visible world have their inner equivalent. The world-soul is supposed to be outside of our concept of space and time. The past and the future, the near and the far are said to be all on the same level. Everything is synchronized and simultaneous. A person who is capable of contacting this world-soul is able to view everything on one level of projection. The mystical participation and union with the world-soul enables such a person to enter into a sphere of higher intelligence where the limitations of space and time no longer hold true.

As dazzling as this hypothesis may be, till now there is no evidence or proof to support the idea of an ethically neutral world-soul. It would be difficult to arrive at this idea even if one had already grasped the concept of hypostasis, that is the personification of Wisdom (chokmah) or of the Word (logos) as we find it in Prov. 8 and John 1. However, in the New Testament the situation is much simpler. We find there that the problem is of a two-sided nature: prophecy is inspired either by the Holy Spirit or by the devil (Acts 21:10, 16:16).

Ex. 131. A farmer's wife had a pain in her right forearm. At first the pain was treated as rheumatism but one day the woman made the interesting discovery that the pain would suddenly subside if she wrote a letter. Having discovered this, whenever the pain became unbearable she would always take a pencil and begin to write in order to alleviate the pain. But after a period of time the woman developed a writing compulsion. She would write things down that she could normally speaking never have written. Added to this the written material on each occasion turned out to be some form of religious treatise. The woman took the articles to her minister to let him examine them. He was surprised at their intellectual content, for the woman had had little or no formal education. By now the originally harmless activity had become a definite habit of automatic writing. One day the name Felix appeared in her notes. It was supposedly the name of a spirit who claimed that the woman had been chosen by God to pass on some special revelations to the world. He announced himself with the words, "In the Name of the Lord Jesus, our blessed and exalted Lord and Saviour", and had then gone on to say that she was to be a prophetess who would bless mankind through her writings. The simple farmer's wife had by now become a spiritistic writing medium.

The parapsychologist would merely see in this example a psychic automation involving the expression of subconscious thoughts. It is true that we need not consider the woman to be in direct contact with the dead, or putting it another way we need not assume that this is a case of direct demonization, but one of indirect demonization. Either way, if the woman were to consider herself to really be a prophetess, then she would have fallen a victim to spiritual pride.

Ex. 132. A Protestant minister took part in a spiritistic séance in order to test the claims of the medium. At the meeting the medium went into a trance, which is a kind of hypnotic sleep. It was then claimed that the apostle Paul was to speak to those present. The minister followed the sermon of the alleged apostle with the greatest of interest. But he was disappointed with the contents. The so-called sermon had little or nothing in common with the letters of the apostle. It seemed to be more the product of the imagination of the medium than of Paul, and it merely consisted of a few moral aphorisms with an admixture of Christian trimmings. The minister was completely unimpressed and was himself convinced that it was a piece of unconscious fraud.

The philosopher Wundt once said, "The great minds must have turned into imbeciles on their passing into eternity, because when they are cited by mediums the things that they say are so dull and trivial." Wundt implied that the mediums were really only producing their own thoughts when great minds of the past were supposedly speaking through them. Any person acquainted with the Scriptures will at once recognize that the apostle Paul would never appear at the citation of a medium.

Ex. 133. A medium was once given the task of materializing the poet Uhland at a spiritistic séance. As it happened a phantasm did in fact appear during the séance. The audience asked it for a poem to prove that it really was Uhland. Instead of reciting a poem the phantasm reached across to a briefcase nearby. Without opening it the phantasm's hand passed through the leather and took out a piece of paper. It then wrote a few lines of poetry down on the paper which still exists today. Later the paper was given to some experts who tried to find the poem among the existing works of Uhland. But they searched in vain. However, a sensational discovery was made. A graphologist confirmed the fact that the handwriting was the actual handwriting of Uhland. Afterwards in Berlin there was even a court case over the ownership of the piece of paper. The court finally awarded it to the medium who is still in possession of it today, as one of his acquaintances told me.

From the scientific point of view it is still not necessary to believe that Uhland really did appear in this case. Depth psychology suggests that a phantasm can be produced in the following way. The medium through emitting energy causes matter to form as a result of this. In nuclear physics we have the idea that matter is nothing more than concentrated energy. Einstein's formula $E=m.c^2$ illustrates this relationship. A comparison can also be drawn from another branch of physics. It is found that both particles and anti-particles are formed at the cathode of an X-ray tube when a current is passed through it at a very high voltage. Energy in the form of electro-magnetic waves is in this way transformed into matter. The next step in the mediumistic process involves the unconscious tapping of the information from some source or other, and then the newly formed matter is psychically shaped according to this information. The final step is made when the phantasm is brought under the control of the medium. Looking at it from this point of view there is no necessity to believe that the dead person has in any way been disturbed. An animistic explanation based on the powers of the subconscious is thus sufficient to explain the phenomenon of materialization. Yet this is not to say that the rationalistic explanation does justice to the facts of the case. The problem is not as simple as that. In this present book though, we have not got the time to delve further into the scientific side of the issue. From the Christian counsellor's point of view suffice it to say that

I have on many occasions witnessed a disintegration of the personalities of both mediums and participants where materializations have taken place. In addition to this in every case where a person has frequently taken part in spiritistic séances, a certain immunizing effect against the Holy Spirit and towards the things of God is in evidence. Contact with the spiritistic world blunts the personality against the power that flows from the Word of God.

Ex. 134. A man stated that he had the clairvoyant ability to find missing persons. A woman went to him taking with her the photographs of her two sons who had been reported missing on the Russian front during the last war. She gave him one of the photographs and having concentrated on it for a while the man went into a trance. He then told the woman that he could not get in contact with the son, and that he was therefore probably dead. She now handed the second picture to the man by way of a check, as it was believed that the second son had indeed been killed in action. However, this time the clairvoyant said, "Yes, I can see your son. He is in a large stone building South-East of Moscow. I can see that he will return home in 1954." The woman found it impossible to believe these statements of the clairvoyant as her son had been supposedly killed in 1943, and she had heard nothing of him since. Her surprise was even the greater when in 1954 this son returned home alive and well. It also transpired that he had in fact been interned in a white stone building unlike the more usual wooden barracks associated with prisoner of war camps.

Parapsychology sees in this example two parallel phenomena. The clairvoyant had the faculty of psychometry, which is the ability to divine by means of an object associated with the person in question, and at the same time he was able to practise the excursion of the soul. This second ability is recognized among the Laps in Scandinavia, and too among the Tibetans. In Europe it is found among the Rosecrucians, some of whose members have this ability and actually use it. Spiritists affirm that there are people who can send out an astral body from their material body, and commission it to do whatever task they will.

Here we shall conclude our round of the principal psychic phenomena of spiritism. One shudders at this dark jungle of human aberration in which spiritism has its haunts. What a contrast we find in the Word of God which bids us to "love the Lord our God with all our heart and soul and mind and strength." Every task that we find to do and all the energies we possess must be directed towards serving our Lord and Saviour Jesus Christ.

(II) Physical Phenomena

Having dealt with the more subjective forms of spiritism we will now turn our attention to the objective physical phenomena connected with spiritism. These include telekinesis, levitation and apports, in which the physical laws of nature are supposedly overcome in an inexplicable manner. Telekinesis means moving an object when some distance away from it without physical aid. The word is derived from the two Greek words 'telos' and 'kineo'. Levitation comes from the Latin word meaning 'to ease' or 'to lift', and its spiritistic usage is that of 'to rise' or 'to float in the air'. The word apport comes from the Latin 'apportare', and is used to denote objects that appear or disappear in a room or a container — usually during a spiritistic séance. We could also include here the phenomenon in which matter is penetrated. With the help of some examples we will now clarify what we mean by these strange events.

Ex. 135. In a secluded mountain village there was a house which was haunted. Various objects used to be thrown through the air and furniture would move around by itself. The local minister, the police and even the mayor and other officials examined the farm house but a complete explanation was never found although it was observed that the telekinetic phenomena only occurred when a fourteen-year-old boy was present. On one occasion a teacher actually saw a heavy oak wardrobe move six feet across a room when the boy was standing nearby.

Ex. 136. A similar example to this occurred at a farm house in an Alpine valley. At first some knocking and scratching noises were heard in the house. Later objects were seen to fly through the rooms for no apparent reason. It was observed that the objects sometimes travelled in a rectangular course which is physically impossible. These events grew even more complicated, and things began to appear and disappear in both closed rooms and containers. A great number of people were by now intrigued by the whole affair and a committee was set up to attempt to discover the underlying cause. The committee consisted of a professor, an electrical engineer and a philologist, the latter being acquainted with parapsychological phenomena. The first thing that they noticed was that the son of the family living in the house was a strong medium. In the course of time he accomplished some astounding feats in the presence of the three men. The most outstanding of these was to lift a bed by means of levitation. This he did on several occasions, and once the boy even succeeded in lifting the bed when the three men were trying as hard as they could to keep it on the floor.

Ex. 137. A woman had some silverware stolen and she suspected a young maid who worked for her and who already had quite a bad reputation. The woman turned to a spiritist for help. This man was both a clairvoyant and a medium, and he also possessed the remarkable powers of materialization and dematerialization. This spiritist went with the woman into the back yard of her house and there put himself into a trance. Suddenly they were disturbed by a strange noise from the roof of the house, and then the stolen silverware fell from the roof on to a manure heap beside the house. The woman had no idea how this apport was accomplished.

One might be able to find a natural explanation for this occurrence, as for example someone throwing the stolen articles out of the skylight at that moment. It could not have been the maid though, for she had already been given notice. But it could have been one of the other employees with whom she had been friendly, and who may have received the stolen articles from her. Whatever the case the following example is even harder to explain.

Ex. 138. This time I was able to investigate the matter myself. The house in question was also examined by some university men, by the police, by both a Catholic and a Protestant minister, by a government official and by others who were merely drawn through curiosity. Over a period of six weeks 135 objects were reported to have flown through the rooms in an inexplicable manner. Each one of these occasions was carefully noted. At the same time several apports were observed. Once when the Catholic priest and two other men were in the kitchen a glass ball came flying into the room, and all the doors and windows had been shut! The ball fell at the feet of the priest who picked it up. It felt hot, but it was undamaged. On the ball was a picture of Maria Einsiedel, a Catholic pilgrimage place in Switzerland. The owner of the house exclaimed that the ball had been in the living room, and so the three of them went to investigate. The ball in the living room had disappeared!

When I examined this case I noticed two things which always seem to occur in conjunction with such events. The appearance of the objects was always connected with the presence of a young boy with mediumistic abilities.

And moreover, magic had previously been practised in the house. When I asked the householder, "Have either you or your ancestors ever practised magic or spiritism here?" he immediately replied that his father had been a cattle charmer and had been able to conjure diseases away. In my own experience, spontaneous apports only occur in the vicinity of a medium, and in houses in which occultism has been practised. In all the cases I have been able to examine, this rule has never been broken.

This last example naturally leads us on to consider the spiritistic-magical phenomena.

(III) Spiritistic-Magic Phenomena

We have seen in the preceding examples that some quite remarkable events are to be found associated with spiritism. One can imagine that in the hands of a person of criminal tendencies such a spiritistic ability would be the cause of much harm. And this is indeed the case. I have been a witness to some terrible examples of this. One of the worst examples I found in a spiritistic circle of some twenty members. The circle used to practise black magic as well as spiritism, and they made experiments to see whether or not they could cause psychic harm or illness to those people they disliked. One of the members of the group, a strong medium, aimed his powers at a minister and stated that he would get rid of him through making him ill. Subsequently the minister had a nervous breakdown and was unable to continue his work over a period of some months. The following examples will help clarify the picture.

Ex. 139. A young woman reported that for several years she had been frightened each night by the appearance of one of her neighbours between 12 and 1 o'clock. Every time this had happened the woman had woken up with a start. She had been terribly frightened. It was not a dream for she had always seen the apparition as she was actually waking up. The phantom was in fact that of one of the women in the village, and this particular woman had the reputation of being an evil person who indulged in plaguing people through black magic. After the woman's death the young woman ceased to have these strange experiences.

Ex. 140. A young farmer had the experience of being beaten up at night in his home. Sometimes he was beaten so much that he actually bled. The whole village had seen him on numerous occasions with black and blue weals across his body.

Ex. 141. A woman came to be counselled and complained of being troubled and disturbed each night by a black cat coming into her room. It had, she said, both bitten and scratched her. I questioned her on whether she had ever suffered from eczema or bad blood circulation, from itching or other diseases such as arteriosclerosis, but she answered to the negative. Concerning the cat though, she said that once when it bit her the wound had not healed for a couple of weeks. On another occasion she said that besides the usual bites and scratches, on one of her legs the number three had appeared as if tattooed with a fine needle.

When approaching a case like this the first thing to do is to eliminate everything of a spurious nature. We know that there are some types of psychiatric illnesses which prompt a person to think in a certain way. For instance many schizophrenics have the idea that they are being persecuted by magic or some other influence. In reality this is only a symptom of their psychotic disease. Nevertheless there are genuine examples of spiritistic-magic phenomena, and I have in my files a lot of first-hand material on which I have been able to form a valid judgement. In the majority of cases a psychiatric explanation involving severe hysteria, onerogenic disturbances or psychogenically based dermographism is not enough. The main reason for saying this is the fact that people suffering in this way are at once delivered when they turn their lives over to Christ and put themselves under his protection. Seen from the parapsychological point of view, magic persecution is a mediumistic problem similar to that of materialization. In the same way that a medium can emit energy that can be transformed into the phantasm of a man, so he is able to transform the same energy into the form of an animal. I have on record many cases of the materializations of dogs, cats, frogs, snakes, and even cases where the apparition was half man and half animal. To show that these phenomena are primarily concerned with materializations we could mention in passing the following fact. If a phantasm is injured in some way at a spiritistic séance then the medium also suffers in a similar way. The same holds true in the case of animal phantasms. We are thus justified in coming to the conclusion that magic persecution is on the same level as materialization. Many methods of defence magic are based on this fact. It is reckoned that if the victim is able to injure the phantasm that is assaulting him, then he has as good as won the battle. We see then that certain forms of spiritistic offensive and defensive magic are based on materializations. Now an example.

Ex. 142. I was told the following story in an area where black magic is frequently practised. A large black cat was found to be hanging around the house in which a woman was about to give birth to a child. The cat would not go away until finally someone threw an axe at it, thereby injuring its leg. Next day it was discovered that an old woman in the neighbourhood had also hurt her foot. The villagers knew this woman to be a master of black magic, and indeed a few days later she took her revenge. On visiting the mother of the new-born child she murmured something and at the same time patted the child on the head. Thereafter the child cried continuously for days on end and could not be pacified. It was also discovered that as the child grew up its memory was particularly weak.

I have in my files about 40 examples involving cats, and almost all of them deal with the same problem, that of a person causing an apparition to appear in a house or a farm. In spite of this, on the whole our universities refuse to recognize events such as these since they are still under the ban of their own rationalistic teaching. The common people are far better orientated with regard to magical customs than those at the universities, for the latter remain disciples of the theory that magic is either nonsense or deception.

However, for the Christian the chief concern is that a person assailed by magic is brought to a point of committal to Christ. Herein lies the only effective means of help. The weapons of our warfare are spiritual and not carnal, says the apostle Paul.

We now come to the fourth form of spiritism which we will be dealing with, and its interpretation and explanation is far more complicated than those listed so far.

(IV) Metaphysical Phenomena

We will be considering under this heading some of the occasions in which spiritism is found in conjunction with ghosts and apparitions of this nature. The problem is many-sided and as with all occult phenomena some of the facts relating to it are genuine while others are artificial and false. Eidetic images and hallucinations belong to the artificial side, and so do visions that one associates with the idea of second sight. Genuine cases of ghosts can be considered to be those which have been objectively confirmed over several generations. I can give an example of this to illustrate what I mean.

Ex. 143. A university graduate, the son of a Protestant minister, told me the following story. His father had once been transferred to take up his ministry in a small town. After the family had moved into the manse they discovered that it was haunted. One night they heard footsteps going from the cellar to the attic and then back again. There were also footsteps in the hall and at first they thought that it was a burglar. On one occasion they even called the police. In addition to the footsteps the lights were sometimes turned on, and the gas too. No amount of careful investigation was able to produce any evidence as to the cause of the apparent haunting. Later, when the two oldest sons were at college they thought of a plan to contact the ghost. One evening the whole family sat around a table and formed a chain with their hands. Their idea was to use table-lifting to communicate with whatever was causing the disturbances in the house. They proceeded to ask some questions: "Are you unable to find any rest?" In response to this question there was a violent rapping on the table. So began an interesting question and answer game. The spirit with whom they had made contact stated that he had been a Catholic priest who had lived in the house 200 years before them. He had murdered his housekeeper and had buried her in the basement. Since then he had had to haunt the scene of his crime. When he was asked in which room he had murdered the housekeeper the table suddenly began to move across the floor. It then hit the door of the room so hard that the wood was chipped. As one of the sons opened the door the table rushed into the adjoining room and slid into the corner. In the course of doing this it hit an oak bedstead so hard that it left a permanent impression on it. The spirit was questioned further and when he was asked if there was anything that could be done for him he replied, "Yes, you can pray for me." The minister's wife did in fact pray for the restless ghost after that, and for a number of years the house was no longer haunted. The son who told me the story and who is now a doctor, went on to say that he had made some inquiries and discovered that a Catholic priest had indeed lived in the house at the time stated, and that the house had been haunted for several generations. It is interesting to note that when the minister moved on to a new appointment he said nothing to the new occupants about the ghost. However, when the family had departed the haunting reoccurred.

There are several ways of explaining the phenomenon of ghosts. Martensen Larsen believes that every man impregnates his own home spiritually. This impregnation, he says, continues to live on in the house after the departure of the person concerned. Professor Gatterer believes that a man does not only leave his physical body behind when he dies but also a spiritual 'larva'. Professor Bender does not go so far as this and only speaks of an eddy current being left behind by the departing person. Spiritualists believe that a man, when he dies, leaves a spiritual complex behind that has an independent existence in the astral world, and which sometimes only disintegrates centuries later. This spiritual complex is supposed to cause the phenomenon of ghosts and apparitions. For some Christians the realm of the dead is not so much a place as a state of being, and some think that there are times, as for example at one's deathbed, when this realm of the dead becomes visible to our earthly eyes. Christian Theosophy suggests the idea that human beings have to remain in the mortal sphere after their death until they are freed from all the things that once tied them to the world. This idea is similar to the popular opinion that criminals and other such people have to haunt the place of their crime until they are taken out of this sphere to a higher or lower level of existence. Yet none of these theories is completely reliable and the Bible itself remains silent on the matter of ghosts. To make one point clear, we would mention that ghosts do not occur only in connection with spiritism, but we have dealt with them here since the problem arose in Ex. 143 where spiritistic table-lifting was used to contact the ghost in question.

Ex. 144. Another minister also moved with his family into a new manse. Again both he and his wife heard ghost like phenomena in the house. At night they heard footsteps about the house and at the weekend of Easter they heard such a lot of crashing and knocking that it sounded as if all the furniture was being smashed to pieces. On investigation they found nothing disturbed at all. The noises continued at other times and several guests heard them although they had never been told that the house was haunted. The minister and his wife prayed continuously about the disturbances and finally he decided to command the invisible powers in the name of Jesus to depart from the house. One morning after this while it was still dark they heard a noise as if all the bricks in the house were being tapped, and this was followed by another noise comparable to hundreds of pigeons flying away. The minister was now convinced that the ghost had left, and this proved to be true for the house was no longer plagued by the noises and disturbances as it had been in the past. Later while investigating the possible causes of the ghost it was discovered that many years previously a spiritist had lived in the house, and on top of this someone had committed suicide there a few years before the family had moved in.

When asked for my advice and thoughts on cases of genuine haunting I always mention two things that constantly reoccur in such instances. Firstly the appearances always have their roots in the occult activity of those who have previously lived in the house, and secondly, although ghosts associated with particular places are more persistent than ghosts or apparitions associated with particular people, the ghost will immediately begin to retreat when people living in the house commit themselves to Christ and put themselves under His protection. This indicates that the occurrences are not to be explained away by some scientific explanation or other, but that a metaphysical answer has to be sought for to understand the whole truth.

(V) Spiritistic-Religious Phenomena

When one seeks to point out the dangers of spiritism by means of the more exaggerated examples one can often be faced with the following response. "But we don't engage in such a primitive form of spiritism as that. We are interested in spiritualism, and that is a noble and a spiritual thing." I was once told by a man who had been a spiritualist for a number of years that he himself considered spiritism as opposed to spiritualism to be a crime.

Well, what is the answer to this question? Has spiritualism succeeded where spiritism has failed? It is true that today spiritualism seems to have taken over from spiritism, and whereas spiritism is concerned with more animistic experiments, spiritualism attempts to take within its scope the religious and the spiritual world. One cannot argue with the fact that spiritualism exists on a much higher level both intellectually and ethically than spiritism. There is for example in Zurich a spiritualistic 'Lodge' which holds services each Sunday in which there are the usual hymns and prayers and sermon. The sermon is allegedly given by a departed spirit from the other side through the help of a medium, and each week it is taken down in shorthand and then published later. I have read several of these sermons and they contain a mixture of idealistic, moral and Christian thought. However, their general standard is far below that of the New Testament. They fail to present the very centre of the Christian message, which is that before God man stands as a helpless sinner who needs the redemption that there is in Christ Jesus. Another point to note is that spiritualists interpret the New Testament in a quite unique way. For example they say that the appearance of Moses and Elijah on the mount of transfiguration, and also the resurrection appearances of Christ, were really materializations which one would normally associate with a séance. As well as this, by means of a forced exegesis of Scripture they avoid the direct command of Deut. 18 and other passages which forbid communication with the dead. Once when I cited this very passage to a member of a spiritualistic church he exclaimed that they did not call on the dead but rather upon living spirits from the realm of the dead. The result of all this is that spiritualism merely confuses people through its apparent Christian façade.

The disastrous thing is that some Christian circles fail to recognize the evils that lie behind both spiritism and spiritualism. This can be shown by the following two examples.

Ex. 145. A Christian family, members of an evangelical church, hold séances together with their aunt acting as medium. In this way some of the well-known Christians of the past have apparently appeared and conducted the meeting, as well as preaching to them. It is noteworthy though, that these 'spirit' sermons contain nothing exceptional, and usually fall well below the standard set by the writings of the men in question.

Ex. 146. A Christian woman lost her husband soon

after their marriage. Nothing would console her in her loss, but later a strange thing began to take place. Her deceased husband started appearing to her at night, and he told her that he had been allowed to do so in order to comfort her in her distress. In this way their marriage was able to continue through these nightly appearances. The woman claimed that she received help and strength from her husband's coming to her, and she used to ask him about any problems that she had to face. A well-known Christian minister advised her to end this communication with the dead, but she could not be convinced that she was in any way wrong in what she did. However, as time went on the woman began to suffer from various psychic disturbances and her health slowly deteriorated.

It is a sad indication of the lack of the gift of discernment of spirits when Christians fail to distinguish between the spiritistic and the Spirit, or between the psychic and the spiritual. It is not enough to say that some great men of the past have witnessed the appearance of the dead, because our standard is not so much the experience of men as the testimony of the Holy Scriptures. When the rich man asked if Lazarus could go back from the dead and visit his friends he was told, "They have Moses and the prophets." We do not need to take our stand on visions or to rely on the confusion which arises from the spirits of the dead. It is to the Bible that we must turn as the Word of God and the purveyor of the Holy Spirit. Again it is not so much the spiritistic writings of certain mediums that we need, as the Spirit of truth found in the written Word of God. This extension of spiritism into the religious world as a religious movement is perhaps the most dangerous aspect of the whole subject. It is through this façade that many simple people are blinded and confused, and hence are led away from the Lord who died for them. But now we come to our final assessment of all the phenomena connected with spiritsm.

(VI) An Assessment of Spiritistic Phenomena

First of all we will hear what the medical world has to say about the problem. It is known particularly in the field of psychiatry that prolonged activity with mediumistic forces produces symptoms of schizophrenia. This has been termed mediumistic psychosis. Psychology too has drawn certain conclusions on the matter, and Professor Bender, a psychologist of the University of Freiburg in his booklet entitled 'Parapsychology — its results and problems', has warned people in these words: "Thousands of people base their hopes on the deceptive statements of spiritistic practitioners and subsequently become dependent upon the advice they receive from the 'other side'. I have quite a number of patients who have suffered serious psychic disturbances through the misuse of such practices. Their personalities have been split and they have been utterly confused by the spirits on which they have called. People therefore who try to discover what life after death is like through spiritism and superstition are in danger of falling prey to the dark and hidden side of their own minds and souls."

Secondly, as we have already seen, the Scriptures are quite clear in their pronouncements against spiritism. To remind ourselves we shall again quote from the books of Leviticus and Deuteronomy. "A man or a woman who is a medium shall be put to death; they shall be stoned with stones, their blood shall be upon them" (Lev. 20:27), and, "When you come into the land which the Lord your God gives you, you shall not learn to follow the abominable practices of those nations. There shall not be found among you any one who practises divination, a soothsayer, or an augur, or a sorcerer, or a charmer, or a medium, or a wizard, or a necromancer. For whoever does these things is an abomination to the Lord. For these nations, which you are about to dispossess, give heed to soothsayers and to diviners; but as for you, the Lord your God has not allowed you to do so" (Deut. 18:9–14). We know too that the prohibition continued on through the Old Testament. Saul himself had banned all mediums and fortune-tellers although when he committed apostasy he sought out a medium in order to know the future. In this way he received his own death sentence, and he died the next day. Later, in the time of the prophets, the warning was repeated over and over again. Spiritism is a sin against the sovereignty and authority of God, and those who trespass into this realm, transgress the commandment, "You shall worship the Lord your God, and Him only shall you serve", which is in effect the first commandment. Spiritists are those who have forsaken the true and the living God to partake and drink of the cup of demons. The following tragic example shows how true this is.

Ex. 147. For many years a Protestant minister was a member of a spiritistic circle. His sixteen year old son also took a regular part in these séances. When his son fell behind in his school work he was given the job as book-keeper of the spiritualistic association. The minister's sermons were often influenced by his contact with spiritualism and contained such remarks as, for example, that the Holy Spirit was merely the good that is in all people. He told his congregation that there are both good and bad spirits on the other side which have a direct influence on our daily lives. He claimed that one can be led and guided by these spirits, and he made no secret of the fact that he himself was so directed. On one occasion however, his so-called leading of the spirit caused him to become the laughing-stock of the whole village. The spirits had told him that his mother had been taken seriously ill. The news soon spread around the village and the minister left at once to go to see his mother. About half an hour after he had left however, a letter arrived from her saying that she was in the best of health. His wife had at once sent a messenger after her husband to tell him the news, and he subsequently returned home. After this experience the village only mocked his ideas about guidance and the spirit world. Later when he and his wife were on holiday he said to her on the beach one day, "I am going to swim out now and I won't come back." He did just that and was never seen again.

Here we see the tragic effects that can result from the confusion caused by spiritism. The minister had dissolved the Holy Spirit into a few moral attributes. He had volatilized the person and work of the Comforter into a few inobligatory human qualities, and instead enthroned his own spiritistic guides. These 'good' spirits had subsequently made him a fool in the eyes of his whole congregation and were also probably responsible for his death.

Thirdly we can turn to the results of Christian counselling work for yet another evaluation of spiritism. As in all cases of occultism we must distinguish between the scientific and the spiritual sides of the problem. One method of investigation deals with the scientific aspect on a material level while the second method of investigation concerns itself rather with the essence of spiritism and how it compares with the Scriptures. The conclusions arrived at in each case will be completely independent of one another, and hence even if spiritism were proved to be entirely explicable in scientific terms the problems raised in counselling work would still remain unanswered. Further research in depth psychology will never be able to replace the Christian's task of counselling those suffering from the effects of occultism. The spiritual side of the problem lies in a completely different dimension to the scientific side.

Pastoral and counselling work has shown beyond any shadow of doubt that spiritistic activity when considered in the light of the Scriptures is one of the places where the powers of darkness invade our lives. I say 'one of the places', for these forces attack us in many other areas of our lives. The warning of the apostle Paul takes on a special meaning for us: "For we are not contending against flesh and blood, but against the principalities, against the powers, against the world rulers of this present darkness, against the spiritual hosts of wickedness in the heavenly places" (Eph. 6:12). It is sometimes quite easy to see this invasion of the powers of darkness when one is counselling people, for there are cases in which a person by simply reading occult literature regularly has suffered from disturbances in his mental and religious life. An example of this:

Ex. 148. A young Christian woman received both sermons and other literature from a spiritistic circle. She thought that the articles were of a Christian character and read them regularly. As a result of this though, she became greatly distressed and began to suffer from attacks of despondency. Not knowing the cause of her troubles she continued reading the occult literature. Then one night she saw a red-haired man in her room with a face that was almost aglow. In addition to this she also began to feel a compulsive desire and urge to destroy things. Once she had the impulse to kill her own daughter in spite of the fact that in her own mind she opposed the idea violently. When she told me all this in a counselling session I immediately advised her to burn all the spiritistic literature.

A psychiatrist would of course tell us that a compulsion neurosis associated with various impulsive actions which occur in both clear and disturbed states of consciousness, is a well-known psychiatric pattern. The hallucination fits into the same picture. But even if we accept such a diagnosis, it is still a strange fact that the illness followed in the footsteps of some spiritistic activity. It was this that triggered off the disease, even if we cannot say that it was the cause. Regarding the hallucination of the red-haired man, it should be noted that spiritistic visions of this nature are quite likely to occur in the course of reading occult literature. Sometimes people mistake these visions for genuine religious experiences. But it is again a case of Satan disguising himself as an angel of light.

In spite of arguments to the contrary counselling confirms the fact that when a Christian gets involved in any form of spiritistic activity his spiritual life can be seriously affected. This is not true for the Buddhist or the Moslem or the followers of other religions like this. These religions are not impaired by spiritism. But spiritism does immunize people against the workings of the Holy Spirit. We must be clear in our minds about the distinction here. A person's religious life is not harmed by occultism or spiritism. Indeed spiritism itself is to a large extent a 'religious' movement. The devil does not take away our 'religiousness', his real desire is to sever us from Christ and to prevent us from following Him. When I therefore hear people say that they gain help in their devotions from some spiritistic circle or other, I readily admit that this is quite possible. The point is that there is a great difference between being religious and being born again by the Spirit of God. It is sad to say that our Christian denominations have more 'religious' people in them than true born-again Christians. Concerning the work of the Holy Spirit and the workings of spiritism I have some examples which portray the difference vividly. Here is one of them.

Ex. 149. Without realizing it a Christian man went to a spiritistic séance. Since he felt uneasy he began to pray silently at the meeting. The group was attempting some table-lifting but were unsuccessful. When the Christian left the room later, though, the table then responded.

Suffice it to say then that Christian work reveals numerous cases of people becoming involved in spiritistic activities where definite psychic disturbances have resulted. Although we have not discussed every aspect of spiritism, we have covered the principle forms in which it appears. We will now turn our attention to the method one should adopt when counselling people who have been burdened through contact with spiritism and other forms of occultism.

(VII) Counselling Procedure

The only way to be really delivered from the power and effects of spiritism and spiritualism is through turning to Jesus Christ. Medicine and psychology do not do justice to the spiritual side of the problem. Because Christ died on the cross and rose again from the dead we need not fear when we seek to counsel those subjected to occultism. Satan and all the hosts of darkness are a defeated foe. Jesus has overcome all the powers of the enemy. The triumphant theme of the New Testament is that "Jesus has disarmed the principalities and powers and made a public example of them, triumphing over them" (Col. 2:15), and the song of the Old Testament is, "The right hand of the Lord does valiantly" (Psalm 118:15). This song was fulfilled in Christ and it was Paul the apostle who summed it up in the words, "Thanks be to God who gives us the victory through our Lord Jesus Christ" (I Cor. 15:57). The salvation and redemption which are in Christ are the foundation of all that we seek to do. Remembering this fact we will now go on to consider the actual course that counselling will usually take.

a) Every person who really wants to be delivered must be prepared to commit his life completely to Christ. There can be no sitting on the fence, no half-hearted decision. A man cannot serve two masters.

b) Secondly, as I have said before, it seems impossible

for a person to be delivered without a complete confession. But this is something voluntary as we see from the New Testament. Nevertheless in over 20,000 cases I have not met with one person who had found deliverance without there having been a thorough counselling session beforehand. James must himself have had some experience of this when he wrote, "Confess your faults one to another that you may be healed" (James 5:16).

c) In some cases it may even be necessary to introduce a prayer of renunciation. It is possible when dabbling with occultism for one to make an unconscious contract with the powers of darkness, and this contract must be broken. This may be done by uttering a prayer of renunciation before God and in the presence of some other person who acts as it were as a witness. It is only necessary to break the contract once. God is witness, and he hears our prayers. The form of the prayer may be, "In the name of Jesus Christ I absolve myself from you Satan, and give myself over to the Lord Jesus, accepting Him as my God and my King." These words in themselves are not a magic formula and need not be adhered to rigidly when counselling people.

d) In yet other cases the counsellor may have to command the powers present in the person to leave in the name of Jesus. The gift of discernment is however, absolutely necessary in such a circumstance as this. We must not misuse the authority Christ has given us. It would be wrong to adopt this procedure in the case of a person who is medically ill. It is possible to make serious and harmful mistakes in this particular area of counselling. If there is any doubt in the matter it is better to refrain from exorcizing. And it is essential for those who are using this authority to be true disciples of Christ. Otherwise serious effects may follow. Another point to remember is that it is generally not wise to lay one's hands on a person who is occultly subjected. Jesus himself only laid hands on those who were suffering from physical diseases. A possessed person was always addressed by a word of command.

e) If any one is delivered from the power of spiritism or occultism, then that person must be sure to continue in reading the Scriptures, in the breaking of bread, in fellowship and in prayers. If after counselling one is again assailed and tempted then one must put oneself both daily and hourly under the protection of the blood of Jesus. This is not an emotional or a mystical notion but a biblical reality. We cannot wage war on Satan with sentimentality. If Satan's attack persists one can oneself command the evil powers to leave in the name of Jesus. As we have said before, for an unbeliever to do this is more than useless, and it may even prove dangerous as we can see from Acts 19:13. An uncommitted Christian can also have no real authority over Satan in like circumstances.

Since evil spirits readily return to their original place of habitation (Luke 11:24—26) any one delivered from such powers must continue to watch with care, taking the whole armour of God as a means of protection (Eph. 6:10—18). Above all one must take the shield of faith and the sword of the Spirit which is the Word of God. When a person is rescued from the power of spiritism he must be on his guard against experiences involving visions and other related phenomena. The returning spirits will often attempt to creep back under the guise of some pious camouflage. It is in this way that evil can often enter unnoticed into one's Christian life.

f) In spite of all that we have said so far there are some cases in which a complete and immediate liberation seems impossible. In these circumstances two things may be necessary. First of all one is advised to form a small prayer group of two or three believers, who will be prepared to meet together at least twice a week in order to pray for the subjected person. "If two of you agree on earth about anything they ask, it will be done for them by my Father in heaven" (Matt. 18:19). Two have more authority than one in the spiritual world. The second possibility is that of prayer and fasting. Jesus once said to his disciples in Matt. 17:21, "This kind never comes out except by prayer and fasting." The group may together fast and pray over a series of days in order to aid the deliverance of the person they are praying for. Yet they must guard against the sin of pride which caused the downfall of the Pharisees. Anyone who stands in the forefront of the battle against Satan must be protected by the armour of God. Many a Christian has fallen prey to the enemy in this battle. The pathway of spiritual pride leads often into the depths of hell.

g) Finally it should be mentioned that since some psychiatric illnesses have symptoms that are similar to those portrayed by a person suffering through contact with occultism, the counsellor must be careful not to trespass into an area in which he is not qualified to work.

We have now come to the end of our discussion on spiritism, but to round off our report we will just briefly mention three cases in which people have both sought and found deliverance.

Ex. 150. A young man tried out some experiments he found in the 13 Books of Moses. We repeat, these books have nothing to do with Moses but are books on magic. The man wanted to see if the charms actually worked, and some of them did. On one occasion he went through the ritual described in the book on how to call the spirit of money. He drew a magic circle on the ground and drew some other magic symbols in the circle. He then used a charm three times in order to invoke the spirit. But no spirit came. However, as he repeated the charm he fell down in the magic circle and lay there unconscious for some time. The result was that for several weeks following this event he was semi-paralysed and drained of all his physical strength and will-power. He wished he could die. In this condition he tried to become a Christian. After several counselling sessions and with the help of a group of Christians praying for him he was delivered. He is still a sound Christian today.

Ex. 151. A young woman accepted the invitation of one of her friends to attend some spiritistic meetings. At first she felt as though she gained something from going along to the meetings but later on she began to notice some psychic changes taking place in herself. She began to suffer from depressions which resulted in her consulting a neurologist. During the course of the treatment she was committed to a mental hospital. But now her condition improved as she could no longer attend the spiritistic séances. At the hospital the chaplain came to see her and through his help and counsel she was able to make a complete recovery. Having come within the sound of the Word of God the young woman had learned to trust and follow Christ. She was released from the hospital within a matter of weeks as cured and since that time there has been no recurrence of the illness.

Ex. 152. During one of my evangelistic trips in Switzerland I was able to trace the history of a woman who had practised almost every conceivable form of magic and spiritism. Her mother had cast a spell over her a birth and during her childhood she had on a number of occasions been cured by means of magic. Her parents had taught her how to practise magic and in the course of time they had experimented with black and white magic, magic persecution, defence magic, fortune-telling, card-laying, palmistry, necromancy and so on. The woman had continued the magic practices after her marriage, but one night she was suddenly troubled and disturbed when she was in the process of communicating with some spirits. She heard noises as if chains were being rattled, together with crashes and sounds of knocking. Her bed began to move up and down repeatedly. At first she did not know whether it was a sign of mental illness or a result of her magic practices. She tried to read her Bible and to pray but this was almost impossible. She was convinced that the source of the trouble lay in some evil power. She went to one of her friends, a Christian woman, and subsequently a group was formed to pray for her. At first she wavered between faith and doubt. She was in a turmoil. She longed to be at peace with God but could not rid herself of a terrible feeling of fear. The battle lasted for two years. In the end she saw a vision of a bowl being passed down to her from heaven. It was full of blood and the words came to her, "This is the blood of Christ which has been shed for you." From that moment her attacks ceased as she believed in her Saviour. Faith in Christ had delivered her. Today this woman continues to praise God for her deliverance and salvation through the shed blood of Christ on the cross of Calvary.

We conclude this chapter on a note of triumph. The gospel is the story of the greatest victory ever won in the course of the world's history. The cross stood at Golgotha as a sign of Christ's victory over death and hell. He has liberated us from the powers of darkness. To come to Him at the cross is to partake in His victory as the Saviour of the world.

Chapter Four

Occult Literature

It would be almost impossible to list all the magic books that are in existence. These books circulate among people like poisonous gases, poisoning their very minds and souls. To name a few of those that exist in Europe we could mention such titles as the Romanus Booklet, The Secrets of Nigromantiae, The Fiery Dragon, The Book of Venus and so on. One could also include under the same heading a lot of spiritistic and spiritualistic literature. However, the principal work on the subject of magic in Europe is the so-called 6th and 7th Book of Moses. The tragedy is that this book is still being printed today. Several court cases have been held in order to attempt to prohibit the sale of this book, but all without success. The details that are recorded in this chapter were used in the legal proceedings of one such case against the publishers of the book. Even if a person is not interested in the history of this book the following examples ought to be read for they will serve as a warning to all those likely to become involved with such literature.

Concentrating then on the 6th and 7th Book of Moses, what is its history? Over the last twenty to thirty years I have had many copies of this book handed to me in the course of my counselling work. The oldest edition that has come into my hands is dated 1503. In the preface of this particular edition it is said that the book was published under the protectorate of the Pope and that the original copy lay in the Vatican at Rome. But statements like this would have to be verified before they could be accepted. In another preface we read that the book consists of charms collected together by a monk from

Erfurt in Germany. If one studies the various editions of this book that date back over the last four centuries, one sees that their contents vary widely.

In the 19th century the 6th and 7th Book of Moses was combined with part of the book The Fiery Dragon. This second book originated in France and is supposed to have been printed at the end of the 17th century from manuscripts dating from the year 1552. After the French revolution in 1789, a revolution aimed at dethroning God and enthroning the goddess of reason, this particular book, The Fiery Dragon, became a sinister substitute to the Bible in some French magic circles. In the history of religion this often happens. Those who repudiate the Living God ultimately fall prey to the devil. After the merging of the two books they came to be published under the new title of The Magically Sympathetic Magazine as well as under their old titles.

The appearance of the name Moses in the original title is only a deception. Moses himself had nothing to do with magic. Magicians however, have tried to elevate him to the position of their patron saint, using as an argument in support of this the fact that he was victorious over the Egyptian magicians in Exod. 7:8. But this is a devilish misunderstanding of the prophetic endowment of this Old Testament man of God. Another thing that can be mentioned is that some copies of this book have an appearance similar to that of a small Bible or a New Testament.

With regard to the distribution of literature of this nature I have over the last few years lectured on the dangers of occultism in England, Germany, France, Spain, Italy, Switzerland, Austria and the Scandinavian countries, and wherever I have gone I have discovered that there exists an extensive amount of occult literature. The 6th and 7th Book of Moses itself seems to turn up in particular wherever one finds German speaking communities, though it is rarely to be found in the new industrialized areas.

To summarize the contents of this and other such magic books is neither necessary nor advisable. Basically it seeks to tell you how to get in contact with the devil. It also contains a wide variety of charms covering magic persecution, magic defence, vengeance magic, death magic, fertility magic, love magic and many other forms of magic. Many of the charms are camouflaged by means of religious trimmings. Any one who desires to read or to keep the book in their house, even for the sake of study, must be warned of the dangers as the book itself promises Satan's special protection to all who read or own it.

Now to some examples drawn from my files. They are mainly chosen at random and could be easily supplemented with many similar cases.

Ex. 153. For a long time a man used to practise the things contained in the 6th and 7th Book of Moses. His wife also shared in his occult practices. What was the result? It is interesting to note that both his children and grandchildren suffer from nervous and psychic disorders. One daughter felt as though a barrier existed between herself and God, and although she later became a Christian she did not even then experience a complete deliverance from her psychic troubles. A granddaughter was to become a Christian social worker but she too felt a similar wall separating her from God. The medical superintendent of a psychiatric clinic told her that her illness was not typical of the usual psychiatric complaints.

Ex. 154. A mother knew of some charms to get rid of warts and skin diseases and she practised them on her children. The children are now occultly subjected. One daughter is a schizophrenic and the mother herself was plagued with blasphemous thoughts and depressions. She said when questioned that she had learnt the charms from the 6th and 7th Book of Moses which her husband had brought into their marriage. In the course of time this woman was shown the way to Christ and she was actually freed from the effects of her charming. On the day that she was converted there were some tremendous crashing and knocking noises heard in the house where she lived, as if the whole house was filled with evil spirits. The mother was delivered, but her children are still subjected to these occult powers.

Ex. 155. A man learnt about black magic by reading the 6th and 7th Book of Moses. He began to indulge in both magic defence and magic persecution, and in the process he used symbolic actions as an aid to the charming. One example of this was that he would stick a knife into a table as a means of protection. Another example was that to plague his enemies he would put some urine into a bottle, seal it, and then utter a charm over it. This was supposed to prevent his enemies from urinating.

Ex. 156. For several years a man practised magic using the same book. Shortly before his death he passed the book on to his eldest son and told him how to use it. The son continued in the footsteps of his father and consequently his children and his grandchildren all suffer from either depressions or melancholy.

Ex. 157. For many years a man followed the instructions of the 6th and 7th Book of Moses and thus experimented in the field of black magic. But the effects of his experiments were clearly visible in his descendants. In addition to this, everyone staying in the house used to hear knocking and rumbling and crashing noises to such an extent that some of the visitors were frightened by them. One of his sons was a very brutal and quick-tempered man who actually brought about his first wife's death. This particular son also used to treat his own children so terribly that none of them would stay with their father when they were old enough to leave home. Even today he continues to treat his second wife in such a way that life is almost unbearable for her.

Ex. 158. Another man all his life indulged in black

magic using the 6th and 7th Book of Moses. His home was a place of unrest and discord. At his death he suffered many agonies and later the house was pervaded by a terrible stench. His wife committed suicide and died in great pain from the poison she had taken. One of their sons died as a young boy and the daughter suffered from serious psychic troubles. Even as an adult she continued to wet her bed and was persistently troubled in her sex life and emotional life. The house in which they lived is now haunted and noises of knocking and rattling are often heard. Ghosts are also seen there quite regularly.

Ex. 159. When she was dying a woman wanted to pass on the 6th and 7th Book of Moses to her eldest son. The son however, refused to accept it. The woman's descendants who did in fact go on to practise black magic included many who were psychically abnormal. Some suffered from melancholy, others from violent tempers, and yet others from extreme forms of quarrelsomeness.

Ex. 160. A man owned and used the 6th and 7th Book of Moses. All his descendants are abnormal. Two of his daughters were for ever going to fortune-tellers and both of them suffered from emotional disturbances. When the man died the house became haunted and a headless ghost was repeatedly seen in it. His grandchildren also suffer from various disorders and one of them as a child always used to fall out of bed. To prevent this the child was charmed. Other grandchildren are today cleptomaniacs and sexual delinquents. A great-grandson at the age of 14 also began to show signs of nervous disorders.

Ex. 161. A certain family used the 6th and 7th Book of Moses for years in order to practise black magic, and now all the children in the family are abnormal. One of the daughters suffers from depressions while one of the sons is an alcoholic and a sex offender.

Ex. 162. I know four ministers who have the 6th and 7th Book of Moses in their libraries. Their reason for this is to be able to study the book for themselves, but it is noteworthy that their congregations are spiritually dead, and this is always the case in such circumstances.

Ex. 163. Another pastor finds his ministry a great burden. His congregation is also known to be both ineffective and spiritually dead. After hearing a lecture on the dangers of occultism this man confessed to having been interested in occult literature for a number of years, and added that he had in his possession a large number of occult books including the 6th and 7th Book of Moses.

Ex. 164. A Sunday School teacher had practised table-lifting for some years. She had also used the 6th and 7th Book of Moses to help charm people against illnesses. In the course of counselling her, I discovered that many people had been burdened through coming into contact with her.

Ex. 165. In 1946 a young man took over his father's farm. That autumn all his pigs died. The cause of death could not be found even though one of the carcasses was sent to the Biological Institute in Zurich for examination. They tried everything but all to no avail. The following year the same thing happened again. This time the farmer redoubled his efforts to discover the cause of the pigs' death. He had the stables inspected and the food analysed but again without success. He thus decided to have the pigsty torn down and rebuilt on another site using completely different materials. Next year the pigs again died. They would all of a sudden squeal and then collapse. The whole process was repeated and every possible examination made in order to find out why the pigs had died. At this time certain of the farmer's neighbours began to say that someone must be killing the pigs magically out of spite. At first he would have nothing of this and continued to seek the advice of the vet and other such people. But they could not help him, and so in the end he went to see the local minister to ask him about the question of magic. The minister simply laughed and said that the idea was stupid. Nevertheless the villagers pointed out to him that there did exist people in some areas of Switzerland who could kill pigs, cattle and horses by means of magic. The farmer could do nothing though, and the event recurred year after year in spite of the fact that by now he had doubly secured his stables with locks and had sometimes stayed up all night with thread stretched out around the house in order to discover if anyone was causing the animals' deaths.

One day, however, the circumstances changed. The minister visited the farmer and asked him to accompany him to the vicarage. There he found one of his neigbours, a man who had a rather poor reputation in the village, and this man confessed that it was he who had been the cause of everything. He had killed the pigs using black magic. The farmer was naturally angry because by now 32 of his pigs had been killed. When asked why he had done this, the neighbour replied that it was because the farmer's children had made such a noise outside his house. He had become so angry that he had tried to get his revenge in this way. When questioned further as to the method he had used, he explained that early in his life he had obtained the 6th and 7th Book of Moses together with several others books on magic. He had studied these books and had later tried to subscribe himself to the devil with his own blood. To do this he had gone out on a Friday night to some crossroads and there drawn up a contract between himself and the devil. He mentioned that the devil had not appeared to him as he is often pictured, but that he met a black curly headed figure with blood-red eyes and a small snout and that the figure had been dressed in rather old-fashioned clothes. Ever since that day the man confessed that among other things he had had the power to kill his friend's pigs. The minister asked him what had made him come out into the open about the whole matter. His answer was that the farmer had been so kind to him over the years that he had felt ashamed and he now asked for the farmer's forgiveness and promised that he would no longer plague him. Not wanting to take any legal action the farmer forgave him and all went well until the neighbour ceased going to church and slid back into his old ways. Since his confession none of the farmer's pigs had died but now as the man again took up his drinking habits two more of the pigs died in exactly the same way as before. Another thing that can be mentioned is that the villagers knew that this man could not only persecute by means of magic, but that he could also obtain money through spiritistic apports.

There is much that can be produced to confirm this report as for example the certificate of the Institute in Zurich. In addition to this the man in question confessed in the presence of two different ministers, and I have myself talked with the veterinary surgeon, who confirmed that he had examined the pigs on several occasions but had found no cause of death. He added that he too had suspected magic. I first heard of the story when the farmer came to me for counselling.

Later, when I visited the farmer again, he told me that he and his wife had now become Christians. He said that they had also started a prayer meeting in their house and that since then, and that was two years previously, no more pigs had died. Christ had overcome the powers of darkness.

We have now to consider the explanation that lies behind these examples. This we can do only briefly, although we are furnished with many clues from the examples we have just quoted.

I repeat that from the psychological point of view it is suggested that a person delving into magic and who believes in occult practices is really only succumbing to a fulfilment compulsion. He unconsciously fulfils the things that he seeks to perform by magic. He is the victim of auto-suggestion. But even if this were the whole explanation as some people affirm, it would still be true to say that occult practices have a corrupting effect on all those who get involved in them.

Again from the parapsychological point of view the examples indicate that whether it is black or white magic which is practised with the help of the 6th and 7th Book of Moses, there are influences exerted on people that cannot be explained merely by resorting to the idea of suggestion. To say as the rationalists do that the whole idea of magic is nonsense is itself untenable. The problem is not as simple as that and the evidence points in the other direction.

Turning to the viewpoint of psychiatry we notice that many families possessing the 6th and 7th Book of Moses are subject to mental illnesses, emotional disturbances and other psychic and nervous disorders. Psychiatrists usually believe that in such cases the cause and the effect have become confused. But again I must point out that I have counselled so many people that I see this cannot always be the case. Often it can be proved that the magic either triggered off or actually caused the psychic disturbances, and some well-known psychiatrists recognize this fact.

In the religious field we note that dabbling with occult literature and occultism results in a resistance to the things of God. This is true whether it is black or white magic, whether it is in a religious guise or not. Basically then we see again that the occult subjection that results from dabbling with occult literature is on the whole a religious phenomenon. As the Scriptures imply, magic is of a demonic character no matter under what name it is known. It is obvious that there is no mathematical proof of this even as there is no mathematical proof that either God or the devil exist. Nevertheless there are many things that point to this demonic nature.

There is another side to magic and magic literature that must be taken into consideration and that is the legal aspect. I have heard of some shocking things in counselling people concerning the effects and results of contact with this field. But as in the case of the pigs, a scientific demonstration of the fact is hard to come by. More often than not one has to adopt a statistical method and rely on the more drastic examples when examining the veracity of magic. The simple principal of cause and effect is hardly ever evident in a tangible enough form to prove by law that magic is the root cause of some offence or crime.

Finally from the aspect of the mental health of a country or a nation as a whole, it would be good if all the literature on magic were to disappear entirely from the scene. Yet this is hardly possible since many families in Europe have books on occultism which they have copied out in longhand themselves. And furthermore, in the case of magic charms, many are passed on by word of mouth from one generation to the next. It would also be advisable to investigate the matter of those who practise magic in a country on a professional basis. It has been estimated that about 90 % of all the people who practise clairvoyance, fortune-telling, mesmerizing, divination and so on, actually depend on occult powers for their profession. The mental and psychic damage done to people as a result of occultism is immense.

In view of the extent to which Europe is infected by occultism and also by the 6th and 7th Book of Moses we see that Christian workers are faced with a double task. One is to enlighten and warn, and the other is to counsel and help those in need. The time has passed in which witches and magicians were either burned or stoned to death. Law as we find it in the Old Testament is no longer the guiding principal in these matters. Our task is not to use force but to produce enlightenment, and the war we wage is to be fought with the help of spiritual weapons. We are to be compared to watchmen and we must not allow our office to be made of none effect through ignorance. We must remember that magic itself is not to be understood by our five senses alone for it is rather a metaphysical and religious and extrasensory phenomenon. Besides warning people, it falls to the Christian to help and care for those already subjected and oppressed by magic. Since occult subjection is a religious issue the treatment is not to be found in psychiatry or psychotherapy. A person who has become occultly subjected has at the same time become the object and target of demonic forces. Help lies neither with the doctor nor with the theologian. It is Christ alone who can help and deliver. The only place where freedom can be found is at the cross of Calvary. It was there that deliverance and redemption was bought for all mankind. Yet to the human mind the cross is a scandal and an offence. Nevertheless deliverance is not so much a matter of reason than faith, as we find it revealed in the New Testament. Faith in Christ overcomes the power of Satan. Christ came as the light of the world and the darkness cannot overcome that light. It was for this purpose that the Son of God appeared that he might destroy the works of the devil. Christ on the cross overcame and conquered all the powers of darkness.

Chapter Five

Miracles of Healing Today

James 5:14–16.

"Is any among you sick? Let him call for the elders of the church, and let them pray over him, anointing him with oil in the name of the Lord; and the prayer of faith will save the sick man, and the Lord will raise him up; and if he has committed sins, he will be forgiven. Therefore confess your sins to one another, and pray for one another, that you may be healed."

Ex. 166. A Protestant minister told me that one day one of the members of his church who was ill had asked if he and some of the church elders would come and lay hands on him and pray for him. The elders however, in every case refused to do as the man asked. None of them had ever done such a thing before and all thought themselves incapable of doing it. The whole idea was completely foreign to them.

Why is this? Why is Christendom so ignorant of what the Bible says about the laying on of hands and prayer for the sick? Why do Christians often lack the courage to put into practice the various passages that refer to healing? Why is it left to the sects and the cults to monopolize these Scriptures? Are these promises only meant for the extremest groups? Is this a sign of the Church's poverty that it no longer lives in the light of the promises of the Bible? These are questions which are relevant today. Let us then consider this problem in the light of the passage we have already quoted from the letter of James, and similar passages.

So as not to make the same mistake that so many of the sects do, we will first look at the actual historical background of the passage in James chapter 5. It was the custom in Jewish communities for the sick to call for the elders to visit them and to pray for them. The early Christians continued this practice although their view of sickness changed somewhat, for they no longer always considered it to be a punishment inflicted on the person by God for some particular sin in his life. The practice of anointing a person with oil was associated in the Old Testament with the choosing of a king and the sanctifying of a priest. It was also a sign of festive joy as we see it expressed in Psalm 23, "Thou anointest my head with oil, my cup overflows." With regard to our text it is also important to remember that oil was considered to be one of the best medicines in existence. This suggests that in spite of the prayers of the elders, medicine itself was not rejected but actually used to combat the disease. It is evident from the Scriptures that oil had both a liturgical and a medicinal use. A parallel can be drawn between the use of oil and the use of saliva. Even today one can occasionally meet this phenomenon on the mission field where in some places spittle is considered to be a person's most precious possession. It is always good, then, to consider the background to the facts recorded in the Bible. Those who claim that a Christian should reject all medical help and who base their arguments on James chapter 5 may find that it is this very chapter that urges us not to neglect the use of medicine. Nevertheless it is true that the passage is in the main dealing with the question of faith healing. Thus if a Christian feels constrained to refuse medical help and to rely solely on the Lord for healing, he cannot be criticized. But such an attitude of faith must never be made into a law which is binding on all Christians. I am sad to say that I know of many unfortunate examples where this has been the case.

One of the most important points to bear in mind when considering the historical background is the fact that there is a distinction to be made between healing motivated by God and magical healing. In the ancient world it was common to imagine that sickness was caused by evil spirits. Hence the process of healing a person was often akin to the exorcizing of demons, and would consist of the exorcizer or the magic charmer calling on the name of the spirit in question or on the name of a more powerful spirit. We have a case of this recorded in Acts 19, where some travelling Jewish exorcists attempted to cast out a demon in the name of Jesus. They themselves were not Christians and the result was that they were overpowered and had to flee. We could easily say that the type of healing recorded in the New Testament is no longer valid for today, were it not for the fact that people claim that similar miracles still happen today. With this we come to the centre of the problem.

It is true to say that almost everyone who falls ill will at some time or other ask himself the question, "How can I get better?" The majority of people will first of all consult a doctor, but if this does not bring the relief they want, many will then turn aside to seek help in occult forms of healing. And these still exist in the 20th century. Times have not changed. In counselling people I have met with a number of different types of occult healing and I want to summarize the more important of these in the following pages.

First there are cases where people have been healed with the help of black magic. It is at once obvious what forces we are dealing with here. An example:

Ex. 167. A woman with mental and psychic disturbances came for counselling. In the course of conversation an amulet was found in her possession. At first the woman refused to part with it because she was convinced that if she did so she would die within a few days. At least this is what the magic charmer had said. Finally however, she handed it over and she was shocked on opening it to find a piece of paper with the words, "My soul belongs to the devil." It turned out that this woman had had tuberculosis, and that she had subsequently been healed by a magic charmer. Nevertheless she parted with the amulet for good. Afterwards her old disease reappeared, yet through putting her trust in Christ and becoming a Christian she was willing to leave her future in God's hands.

In the case of white magic it is not always so easy to see its true nature. This form of magic is more widespread than black magic, the reason being that it often hides itself behind a religious exterior. Hence as we have said before, one needs to have great discernment in these matters in order to recognize the forces that are actually being called into play. The religious trimmings can be very deceptive. Again an example:

Ex. 168. A woman was told by a hospital that she would have to have her leg amputated. Because she wanted to save her leg at all costs she went to visit a magic charmer without the doctor's knowledge. This man told her, "You will have to believe in me if you want to be healed." He went on to repeat a magic charm and then said the Lord's prayer three times. The woman's pain immediately vanished and when she returned to the hospital it was no longer necessary for her leg to be amputated. The doctors were puzzled. Later however, the woman began to suffer from various psychic disturbances and her family too became accident-prone after this.

We repeat, white magic is more often than not accompanied by certain symbols that may include the use of the names of the Trinity, three Lord's prayers, three verses of Scripture, three psalms, or three crosses and so on. People are thereby deceived and the method of healing is thus often mistaken for true Christian healing. In reality however, the third commandment is being broken, which says, "You shall not take the name of the Lord your God in vain." Man cannot dictate to God, and man cannot treat God as a servant who is willing to jump to the aid of every magic charmer who so invokes Him. The Bible relegates both charming and the mechanical use of the Scriptures themselves to the level of sorcery, and so we find that white magic is merely black magic under a different guise. Satan is indeed transformed into an angel of light. The sense of compulsion connected with white magic is something quite different from the attitude of faith in the Christian who says, "Thy will be done."

Prayer which is offered on a professional basis is a third form in which one can find magical healings. Another example will illustrate this.

Ex. 169. A business man suffering from an organic disease consulted a man who offered to pray for his healing on the payment of a small fee. A few days later the sick man visited some friends and complained that he could no longer pray. "I have a feeling as if there is something evil around me", he said. He tried to read his New Testament each day but failed to do so. He was again driven to seek the help of his friends and told them, "You must help me because there are evil forces plaguing me. I've never experienced anything like this before in all my life." And so it continued for several months. The organic disease had disappeared but instead he had symptoms of a mental disease. Finally he was driven to commit suicide, although he was the father of four children. If this were only an isolated case, then the evidence would not be conclusive, but I could add thousands of cases to support the conclusion that the devil is at work behind these supposed healings.

We have already mentioned mesmerism and this constitutes another healing movement which the layman finds difficult to assess. Dr. Trampler still experiences amazing successes on his patients almost every day. In some cases chronic organic diseases have been healed over night. We must ask ourselves on what principles this new healing movement is founded. Dr. Trampler speaks of an animated power which flows through him to his patients. To improve the reception of these powers he has sometimes asked his patients to raise their fingers into the air or to wear some aluminium foil close to their bodies or even to place some under their pillows at night. From the religious point of view there are many different ideas involved here. Trampler himself believes that all the great religions including Christianity are in fact revelations of God. This means for instance that Buddha and Christ are on the same level from his point of view, and it is a question of Buddha and Christ rather than Buddha or Christ. Here he errs from the clear teaching of the New Testament. His healing is therefore a mixture of pantheism, mysticism and natural religion together with a few Christian elements. This is dangerous. We have already pointed out in Ex. 74 the difference between a real faith in Christ and this man's healing abilities. The fact that Dr. Trampler was unable to heal the woman seemed to be vitally connected with the fact that she prayed before he attempted to heal her. This agrees with my observations in other cases involving magic healings.

A fifth method of magic healing is that associated with spiritism. The following example was reported to me by a student.

Ex. 170. An unqualified British doctor went to Germany to demonstrate his methods there. He worked for a time in Heidelberg and he claimed that a surgeon had appeared to him from the dead and given him the ability to operate on and to heal the body. Since this alleged appearance the man has carried out a number of fictitious operations and he is in fact supposed to have had a lot of success. There is no end to the things that people will believe in their superstition. With regard to the student who told me the story, the doctor had had no success when attempting to heal him.

Christian Science is in a certain sense another healing movement. It is not possible to describe this movement in detail here but I will mention a few points that are worth noting. Mary Baker Eddy who founded this particular sect taught people that sickness and death are only illusions and not realities. Man is able to overcome the error of disease through the creative and divine spirit that dwells within him. The dream of death can be done away with through the mind. Because of her teaching many of her followers thought that she would never die. This was of course a vain hope. Yet the effects of her work as we find it in the Christian Science movement can be illustrated by the following example.

Ex. 171. A young man had a plaster cast on his leg. A Christian Scientist visited him and told him that the fracture he had was unreal. He said that he should take the plaster cast off and go home. It was all an illusion. Although this particular member of the movement must have had a very primitive outlook, he had nevertheless hit upon an essential aspect of their teaching when he gave the man this odd piece of advice.

There are yet other strange healing movements in the world today and their number seems to be on the increase. We live in an era of human history in which the uncontrollable forces of the devil are gradually being given more and more freedom. One sensation follows hard on the heels of another. Some examples.

Ex. 172. It is reported that in Syracuse in Italy a wooden picture of the Madonna actually cries real tears which have the power of healing people. I was once able to visit Sicily and saw this Madonna. Every three months tears come from the picture and at such times many people are said to be cured. It is calculated that over the last few years about 800 people have already been cured.

Ex. 173. In America the late Father Divine, the leader of a certain sect, declared that he himself was God, and that his son was Christ. They were both supposed to have the ability to heal and to kill people even if the people were some distance away. A foreign evangelist once told me that his own mother had been killed by this Father Divine through black magic.

Ex. 174. There is a report from the Near East that Prince Abdul, a relative of the late ex-King Farouk, can perform miracles. It is said that he has caused fire to come down from heaven in much the same way as Elijah did, and that he has been able to imitate the miracles of Christ by healing people and raising some from the dead.

Ex. 175. In the South of France, George de Montfavet claims to be Christ, and hundreds of miracles are quoted in support of this claim.

Mankind rushes today from one sensation to another, as a scintillating parade of miracle workers, healers, and saviours dances before its eyes. One wonders if there is anyone left who can still discern the truth from the error.

The question of discernment is of great importance especially in the field of miracles. There are some miracle healers whose work is so hard to evaluate that Christians are often in doubt as to the forces behind these people. We have today for example such men as Tommy Hicks, Harry Edwards, T. L. Osborn and William Branham. Each one of these men depends on mass meetings which are followed by a call to people to step forward for healing. I have over the years collected a lot of information on these particular people and the conclusions that I have come to are not based on any superficial judgement of the matter, neither are they promoted by an attitude of negative criticism on my own part. I have examined cases of healing reported by them and have heard them personally, and compared their teachings with the Holy Scriptures. My aim is to obey the plain words of the Bible, which tells us to "Test the spirits to see whether they are from God." It is again impossible to go into the matter in detail but we will deal with a few of the points which arise in this field.

Without a doubt the man who poses us with the most problems is Branham. He not only exhibits abilities of fortune-telling, mesmerism, and magic but he also has certain Christian characteristics. His whole work is hidden behind a screen of Christian words and phrases. Both his parents believed in fortune-telling and he was burdened through occultism at an early age. He once told an audience in Karlsruhe that he had had visionary experiences since childhood. I was there at the actual time he said this. My comment is that the gifts of the Spirit are not imparted to a person at birth, but they rather receive them after their spiritual rebirth.

Ex. 176. While Branham was holding a campaign in Zurich he called a young man to the platform. He then asked the man, "Do we know each other?" "No", was the reply. Branham went on to say, "Have you got a letter in your pocket from a young lady?" This time the answer was, "Yes". "There is a picture with the letter." "That's right." "Will you show me the picture?" The young man pulled it out and Branham held it up for all the audience to see. "Am I not a prophet of God?" he called out. There was an enthusiastic response from the people together with cries of 'Hallelujah' and 'Praise the Lord'!

But we ask, is a piece of fortune-telling proof of one's prophetic ability? There should be no confusion here. Fortune-telling, as the Bible points out, is of the devil (Acts 16:16). Prophecy is of the Holy Spirit (Acts 21:11). Why was Branham so anxious to demonstrate the fact that he was a prophet? Why does he use a fetishistic custom in some of his meetings in order to bless the sick? That is, why does he pass handkerchiefs around after having blessed them so that those who are sick can hold them to their bodies? One cannot argue that this is to be compared to the practice described in Acts 19:12. Why too is Branham often completely exhausted after his meetings? Jesus and the disciples were never led away in such a manner after they had engaged in healing people. In this respect Branham behaves like an exhausted mesmerizer. And finally, why is Branham's healing ministry disrupted when Christians pray at his meetings? Once he said at a meeting that there was something hindering the proceedings, when unknown to him there were some Christians scattered among the congregation who were praying, and asking God to make His will known to them. Branham's reaction was similar to that of Dr. Trampler. The conclusion that one is forced to draw from the evidence that we have listed here is that Branham is occultly subjected. He has mediumistic abilities. When he became a Christian in his early years he must have dragged these abilities into his Christian life. Today both he and his followers mistake these abilities for the gifts of the Holy Spirit and so the effect of his ministry is to divide and to confuse Christians. Therefore one is to be warned of his ministry. It is significant that Billy Graham and others like him have disassociated themselves from Branham and his movement.

Concerning Hicks it can be mentioned that whereas Branham's work is of a mediumistic nature there are signs that Hicks' is rather of a suggestive character. His healings can often be described as psychic shock effects. An example:

Ex. 177. A university graduate who had studied psychology suffered from chronic paralysis. After a healing session with Hicks the paralysis was cured somewhat but over the next three weeks it slowly returned again. The patient considered the brief improvement to have been the result of suggestion. So it is that as with Branham, suggestive and psychic influences are mistaken for the workings of the Holy Spirit. I repeat that one reason for this is that these men practise behind a camouflage of Christian words and phrases.

With that we have completed our brief survey of the various healing movements that one finds in the world today. We have covered healing as it occurs in conjunction with black magic, so-called neutral magic, white magic, Christian Science, and other movements that fringe on the Christian realm. We again ask ourselves what conclusions can be formed about these movements when we consider them in the light of the Scriptures and in particular in the light of James 5? In many ways they are symptomatic of a condition spoken of in the Bible.

Today we live in a time when the mystery of iniquity is already at work (II Thess. 2:7). Jesus predicted that many false Christs would come, who would lead many astray through demonic signs and wonders (Mark 13:22). The way in which this is happening today is alarming and is evidenced by the fact that many Christians are getting involved with the occult field and with occult healing methods. Time and time again they are being deceived by the religious camouflage.

Healing movements are also a sign of the failure of the Christian Church to meet the spiritual needs of the day. The root cause of the world's problems is that people put their material welfare before their spiritual welfare. The Church has followed the world in this respect and is no longer prepared to launch out in complete dependence on the promises of God. It follows that the counsel of the majority of Christians is not what it ought to be, although the Word of God still offers genuine and effective help to those who are prepared to stand on its promises.

In James we find a crucial point mentioned with regards to healing. He links it with both confession of sin and forgiveness. In the New Testament healing and forgiveness are inseparably bound together, and it is forgiveness that takes pride of place. This is best illustrated in the example of the lame man (Mk. 2). When these two ideas are separated one falls into error. In the case of magical healing the only concern is for the body. Here the motto is, "If it helps, why worry?" But in the Scriptures the primary concern is for the inner man. The body is of secondary importance, and bodily health is not spoken of as essential. Sometimes the Lord allows his children to go through suffering in order that they may increase their patience and faith. We will thus conclude this chapter with an example which demonstrates how a young woman was healed following the confession and forgiveness of her sin.

Ex. 178. The young woman suffered from a throat infection and from a tumor which was about the size of an egg. She had found no relief from her complaint by going to the doctor and a neurologist, and so she finally came for Christian counselling. It was then that she admitted that she had sinned against her husband while he had been away from home. By faith she committed her life to Christ and asked Him for forgiveness. Her husband returned home only a short while after this and with no compulsion she returned with him and repeated her confession. This was completely on her own initiative. Her husband forgave her and within three days the throat infection disappeared together with the tumor. The cleansing of her spiritual life had been followed by the cleansing of her body.

In the New Testament we find that this process is one of the basic elements of the Kingdom of God. Anyone who has experienced a spiritual resurrection in Christ and who now lives by the faith of the Son of God is able to stand on the promises of James 5:14 and Mark 16:17. "These signs will accompany those who believe . . . they will lay their hands on the sick, and they will recover."

The errors and evils of magic and spiritism must not be allowed to obscure the facts of the Scriptures that apply to bodily health and healing. Where the sin of magic and sorcery abounds there the grace of Christ does much more abound.

In conclusion we will once again briefly compare the two basic forms of healing. The Bible does indeed recognize the efficacy of magic. We have only to remember the Egyptian magicians or Simon Magus to prove this fact. Magic can indeed bring a certain relief to the body, but this is a form of short circuit, because the soul of the person is completely bypassed. With the Scriptures the soul obviously takes precedence over the body, man's relationship to God is of far more importance than his bodily welfare. In magic the question is, "What can help?" whereas in the New Testament the question is rather, "Who can help?" The sorcerer will say, "It helps." The Christian says, "HE helps." Behind the 'What' and the 'It' of magic lies the twilight world of uncontrollable powers and forces. It is here that Satan hides himself. Behind the 'Who' and 'He' of the Christian faith stands Christ, the living Word. "The Lord will raise him up," declares James through faith and in gratitude and joy. This same Jesus is the same yesterday, today and for ever. And we are debtors to Him. We owe Him our lives out of thankfulness for what He has done for us. He is the Saviour of the world.

Chapter Six

Genuine Cases of Healing and Deliverance

1. Christ is the Victor

In 1935 I took part in a mission in France. After one of the meetings a man came up to me with his wife and son. He went on to recount the following story: They came from a farm in the Vosges Mountains and for many years their farm had been haunted. Furthermore some of their cows suffered periodically from symptoms of paralysis and the man too had suffered in the same way. No explanation could be found for these facts, neither could it be explained why the cows were often disturbed in their stables and showed signs of great fear. The man's father had once had to sell all but one of the cows because of this trouble, and had been left in a state of near bankruptcy. It was then that his father had gone to a man who had practised witchcraft. After this man had gone through a series of strange ceremonies around the stables, the disturbances disappeared for a while.

Then came the First World War. The family had been forced to evacuate their farm for a number of years and the sorcerer had been called up to do his military service. During this time the man who was telling me the story had married. They had later returned to the farm, but the disturbances had started all over again. Their two children were also both plagued by strange attacks. Another magic charmer had been called in to help the oldest child but the second child had died at the age of six weeks in great pain.

The man himself was plagued in much the same way and in spite of prolonged medical treatment in hospital there was no improvement in his condition. At night he had experienced a feeling as if a strong pair of hands were lifting him up into the air and throwing him down on to the bed again. Added to this the house had been filled with a series of noises, and one could sometimes hear the sound of doors opening and closing throughout the house. There was a strong smell also which nauseated the whole place. The man, having grown thin and emaciated, subsequently sought refuge in prayer, but he had again been shaken by an unseen power. Once, although he had been in a very weak condition, he had managed to get out of bed and taking an old prayer book he had sat down at a nearby table to call upon God to help him. Suddenly a tremendous force had gripped the lower part of his body and he was lifted up and thrown down again on his chair with such force that he thought he would burst.

As a final resort they had called in another magic charmer to help them and after they had taken his advice the conditions did in fact slowly improve. Some time later however, trouble broke out on the farm again, and the cattle were once more plagued and the fields became unproductive. Later still their remaining son fell victim to the strange attacks which he had experienced previously in early childhood.

The farmer's faith in magic charmers had by now diminished and so he consulted several doctors, but all to no effect. When his son had reached his fifteenth year he began to experience even worse things and had seen monstrous figures walking around the house. One morning as he was getting up he had been seized by some invisible force and the result was that his right hand had been completely paralysed. Again medical treatment failed to produce any signs of improvement.

As the man was telling me the story, I noticed that his son's arm was hanging at his side totally lame and limp. It became clear on questioning them further as to what lay behind the unhappy events. It was then that I told them of the terrible consequences of sins associated with magic and sorcery, and I challenged them to repent and to turn to God with their whole heart. I was able to show them, by referring to the Scriptures, that in a case such as theirs it was not a doctor who could help, but only Jesus Christ. It is He who has destroyed the works of the devil. He alone is victor. Both of the parents and the son expressed their desire to repent and to commit their lives to the Lord. In the case of the son I prayed over him in the name of the Lord and by the grace of God he was healed. A few days later he was even helping his father in the fields. From that time God's peace rested on the farm and the stables.

It so happened that later during the Second World War when my own family was evacuated from Strasbourg we found shelter with these same people in their mountain home. We discovered that the Lord Jesus Christ had been glorified amongst them and that they had continued to experience the peace and the grace of God in their house and home.

Henri Waechter, an evangelist from Strasbourg.

2. *The Bulwarks of Darkness*

It was in Hesse in 1938 that I had one of my most memorable counselling experiences. We were holding a mission there when a young man came to me and unburdened himself. His case was so typical that I told him at once that either he or his family had been engaging in occult practices. He admitted this freely and what he went on to confess left a deep impression on my mind. What I am about to write will in no wise break any seal of confession, as the man himself asked me to use his experience wherever possible to warn people of the dangers of occultism.

Let us begin the story, then. Even as a child the young man had suffered from depressions and had had thoughts of suicide and other psychic disorders. From his early years he had heard noises during the night and had sometimes witnessed ghost-like appearances, which had caused rustling and whistling noises. A psychiatrist would perhaps diagnose these experiences as psychoneurosis, but this would not explain the cause of the disturbances. However, when one went into the family history the source became clear.

The young man's great-grandmother had been a magic charmer. She had healed both animals and people by means of her charms. In addition to this she had also belonged to a spiritistic circle which practised communication with departed spirits. It was her involvement with occult phenomena that brought about the tragic downfall of the family.

The magic practices of the great-grandmother had been passed down to her son and daughter, who in turn had charmed both animals and people, using the 6th and 7th Book of Moses as an aid. They had also carried on communication with the dead, and had practised the use of a pendulum and the laying of cards as a means of fortune-telling. They both died in a terrible way. The woman had at night seen ghosts in her room, and she had had the feeling that evil spirits were for ever trying to keep her mouth and nose shut. This continued for many years and finally she had been committed to an asylum. Since she was not really mentally ill though, she was released after six months. Her brother later died in terrible agony in spite of the fact that he had asked that all his magic books be burned or thrown out of the house. He had even asked for a Bible to read, but he was not able to understand it. When he finally died in great pain an obnoxious stench spread throughout the house.

The grandchildren were no better off. One granddaughter used to have fits of frenzy in which she threw furniture around or sometimes lay down in the street screaming almost unbearably. She too was committed to an asylum. Another granddaughter heard the already mentioned sound of knocking during the night, and she was so emotionally disturbed that one day she killed both herself and her two children by jumping with them off a cliff. A grandson became a medium for a spiritistic séance, and he too suffered from a persecution mania and finally ended up in a mental home.

Among the great-grandchildren, one girl continued the card-laying and charming tradition and later died when she was quite young. Her family asserts that she still haunts the house in which they live in the form of a poltergeist. It was one of the brothers of this girl who had come to me for counselling. He told me that he was utterly convinced that all the terrible psychic disorders in his family history could be traced back to their contact with occultism. We see evidenced here the punishment for sin mentioned in the second commandment, ". . . visiting the iniquity of the fathers upon the children to the third and the fourth generation of those who hate me." And this is not an isolated case. In my missionary work I have heard many similar family histories while counselling people. It is distressing to note how little is known of the powers of Satan among psychiatrists and Christian counsellors. The present atmosphere of rationalistic thought has caused these things to be regarded lightly as if they did not exist. But if it is our desire to help people then we must take these satanic forces seriously. Man stands in the midst of a battle between

Christ and Satan. When people think of Satan merely as a man with a tail and horns, and just mock at the idea of a real devil, they make a terrible mistake and thus enable Satan to ensnare and attack his victims without hindrance. The most dangerous area of satanic seduction is magic, for it is here that people consciously participate in Satan's work even though he hides behind a camouflage of pious ceremonies.

Thank God that Satan has not got the last word in this matter. Jesus Christ came to destroy the works of the devil (1 John 3:8). We have a mighty enemy but an almighty Friend, as the late German evangelist, Ernst Modersohn, used to say. The right hand of the Lord does valiantly in all circumstances, even in the case where a person has been driven into direct dependence upon the devil through occupation with occult things. This fact was revealed in the case of the young man whose story I have just recounted. Christ gave him both joy and freedom. The bulwarks of darkness yielded to the almighty hand of the Victor of Calvary. Jesus Christ remains today the Saviour of the world.

3. The Works of the Devil

A woman who was physically and mentally quite healthy began to have an ever increasing number of strange experiences at night. Although there was no one in the room she would have the feeling as if she were being beaten. In the morning she used to have bruises all over her body. This experience would repeat itself about twice a week and she could think of no way of explaining the puzzling events. At first she was rather ashamed to talk about these nightly attacks but in the end she was forced to go to her local minister for advice. He himself could not help her, and even when the woman consulted another minister, still no solution could be found. Since in all other areas of her life she was completely normal no explanation was forthcoming.

One day however, a friend of mine who has a knowledge of the effects of occultism, visited the woman. Since he too could see that it was not a case of mental or emotional disturbance, he asked her if she had had any contact with the occult field. It was then that the following story came to light. As a young girl the woman had been courted by a young man, but she had finally broken off their relationship because she had been unhappy with the man's attitude. After this he had threatened her and said that he would plague her because she had refused to marry him. The woman had thought little of the threat at first and it was only after the nightly attacks had begun that she was reminded of the man's words. But she found it impossible to believe that there was any connection between the two events.

Before we go on with the story I would like to point out that when I am faced with a case such as this, the first thing I do is to see if there are any medical or psychological causes behind the experiences. If this turns out to be the case I send the patient to a believing Christian psychiatrist. Since many puzzling occurrences can now be explained and understood by the recent findings of depth psychology, one must exercise extreme caution when seeking to diagnose troubles of this nature. A wrong diagnosis can have disastrous effects. However, if one is sure that it is not a medical case, one can then turn to the findings of parapsychology and occultism to see if there is any connection to be found there. There is still much that remains unrecognized by our doctors, psychologists and theologians who rely solely on their university education for their knowledge. Occultism still plays a great part in our world today.

Concerning the woman of whom we were speaking my friend prayed with her and encouraged her to put her faith in Christ in order to find complete deliverance. It was during this time of counselling that the man who had threatened the woman hanged himself. The woman was at once freed from the attacks and the experiences never recurred.

This example belongs to the controversial field of mental suggestion, which just cannot be explained away by saying that it is all nonsense. It was Schopenhauer who said, "There is also a sceptism of ignorance." There are still many things between heaven and earth of which the world has never dreamed, as Shakespeare aptly said. Mental suggestion often crops up in connection with the 6th and 7th Book of Moses and I know of enough cases of it to be assured that it is not just a popular superstition.

Even if with the woman the nightly disturbances had been the symptoms of hysteria, the sudden and lasting healing would still be quite extraordinary. Every doctor knows how difficult it is to heal such illnesses. But here we had in fact a magic influence rather than an illness. The Christian is well aware of the fact that we are all surrounded by the hosts of wickedness. Christ would never have come to this world if the devil had merely been the delusion of an unenlightened time. No, the powers of darkness are a present reality. Yet Christ has overcome Satan in his battle for mankind. Christ has destroyed the works of the devil.

4. *Incurably Insane*

A Christian man once told me the following story. His great-grandparents had practised magic. As a result of this his grandparents had developed mediumistic abilities. His grandmother had suffered from depressions and had

had an irritable and selfish nature. Her psychic disturbances had finally led to her being committed to a mental hospital. The trouble reappeared in the next generation, in the generation of the man's parents. When however, the man's father actually turned to Christ all the symptoms of compulsion and other psychic complications disappeared. The man himself had suffered as a child from depressions but when he too became a Christian he had been completely delivered. But it was concerning his son, the fifth generation, that he gave me a really detailed account.

The father told me that the son had been quite a normal child up till the age of eighteen. It was then that the disturbances of his ancestors began to appear. At first it had only been a matter of depressions, but later on he began to fear life itself. His depressions would come and go and would be followed by times of various obsessions. He would have to kneel and pray for hours and then have fits of frenzy in which he would beat his own parents. After such outbursts he would run off into the woods and roam about for days on end until he finally collapsed of exhaustion. He was usually brought home by the forestry workers. Because of the condition he was in, he lost his job. The next step was that symptoms of schizophrenia appeared, and he would hear noises in the house and also see lights and hear voices which told him not to obey his parents. It was under these conditions that his parents were compelled to send him to see a psychiatrist who diagnosed him as being an incurable high-grade schizophrenic who needed to be committed to an asylum.

Instead of taking the psychiatrist's advice, however, the father got some of his friends together in order to pray for his son. He also took the boy to a Christian convalescent home and there he was counselled and prayed with every day. At first the effects were negative and the patient was plagued with religious delusions. He would kneel at a bench in public for hours and pray, and this happened not just once or twice, but many times. Then a second prayer group was formed for him at the home, and after a few weeks a slight improvement was visible. At the end of six weeks the young man's mind suddenly became completely clear at one of the counselling sessions. His compulsive behaviour stopped immediately and after another two weeks he was allowed to go home as cured. He was able to take up his old job again and today he is the chief construction engineer of a large firm and continues to live the life of a truly born again Christian. A man, who in the eyes of the psychiatrist was incurable, had been healed by the power of Christ.

There are two things that come to light in this family's history. The first is that following the practice of magic by the ancestors, the descendants suffered in many ways from emotional and psychic disturbances. The second fact is that when any of the people involved turned their lives over to Christ they were freed from the powers that had once held sway over them. The power of Christ to perform miracles is not dead. Where medicine fails Christ can still be of help. With God there is no such thing as a hopeless case. A doctor who had practised a lot amongst Christians once remarked, "One must always be careful when making a diagnosis in the case of a Christian. Even if today they are at death's door, you may tomorrow meet them at your door both happy and well. Their faith results in the unpredictable, and well-established medical concepts can often go by the board. You never know where you are with such people."

5. Remember not the Sins of my Youth

A young man from Switzerland who had been a Christian for several years wrote his testimony out for me in the following words:

When I was fifteen years old, having a number of warts on my right hand I was charmed magically, as was the custom in the district in which I lived. The result was immediate success. Nevertheless although I was free of the warts I had now placed myself under the ban of magic. Over the next few years the effects of this charming became evident in my life and I became addicted to cheap literature, films on the subject of sex, and other such sexual activities. I rebelled against God and my mind became poisoned by all the evil of my sensual nature. I could find no freedom from my sexual appetite and although I became filled with a feeling of disgust, sin's power overcame me again and again. At this time I was a great burden to my parents and I found it almost impossible to concentrate on my job.

This state of affairs continued for many years until a longing for a freedom from sin was awakened in me. I was invited to go to a men's meeting and the speaker talked on the subject of the things that had caused so much trouble in my life. He pointed out that liberation was available for all who would trust in Christ as their Saviour. I was greatly disturbed but I was too ashamed to seek counsel that night. I sought freedom in other ways and married a woman who already had three children. But it was of no avail. I grew only more miserable. Everything I did disgusted me. Where would it all end? Only God knew.

My wife became ill and I too had to be confined to bed. The doctor could find no explanation for the strange neurosis that overwhelmed me. I almost despaired. A terrible fear began to take hold of me and I thought that I would never get well again. It was then that I started to call on God in prayer. Again and again I asked him for forgiveness and deliverance and finally it became clear to me that I would never be able to deal with all these problems alone. My complete inability to do anything was revealed to me. Then a friend of mine gave me a tract. It was just at the right moment. I was at my lowest ebb and I felt that God had sent the person to me. He is the world's best psychologist. I opened my heart to my friend and confessed the sins of my past life. This was the turning point.

A great joy flooded my soul, a joy of sins forgiven, a joy of real salvation. The words, "If the Son shall make you free you shall be free indeed," had by God's grace become true for me. The Psalmist's prayer, "Remember not the sins of my youth" had been answered in my life. Some words that I had learnt as a child now returned to me in their full force, "In Him we have redemption through his blood, the forgiveness of our trespasses, according to the riches of his grace" (Eph. 1:7). These words were now a reality to me for the first time in my life. God gave me the assurance that they were eternally true. After years of misery I now knew something of Jesus' words when he said, "I am come that they might have life, and that they may have it more abundantly."

6. Jesus Christ Redeems

I was brought up in a family which continually turned to the occult world when sickness or disease raised its head. Although the men we consulted practised under the names of mesmerizers, nature healers, spiritual healers and so on, and although they disguised their work behind a cloak of religion, in reality they relied upon magic charming to achieve their results. The majority of them were very prosperous in their lucrative business, and some even had a name for being practising Christians. Yet the enlightened would have had no difficulty in seeing they derived their powers from the devil and not from God. It cannot even be said that they rely upon neutral forces of nature, although this is what they would like people to believe. No, they work hand in hand with the powers of darkness. I have seen too much of the effects of their work to be persuaded otherwise.

For thirty years my own father practised magic healing himself. He could use his powers on animals and humans alike. Many people used to come to him for help and often only a letter or telephone call was necessary to bring about the required result. This type of healing is going on all over the world and it is not always just a matter of suggestion or hypnotism, but magic and demonic powers also play a part. The effects of my father's charming were visible in our family, and our home was characterized by quarrelling and frayed tempers. In spite of this, after my father's death I endeavoured to learn the art of healing which he had possessed. I was fascinated by the whole idea, and the thought of lording it over people was high in my mind. Because of my contact with my father and the mediumistic abilities that I had already received from him, success came quite quickly to me. At first I used to practise on the rest of the family and later I turned my attentions to our relatives. The more successful the charming was, the more I was filled with pride.

But I too could not avoid the effects of dabbling in magic. Quite unexpectedly I had a nervous breakdown. I had to give up my job and for weeks sat at home doing nothing at all. It was then that God started to speak to me. At this time I met a man who was also acquainted with the idea of magic charming. He warned me of the dangers of contact with occultism and questioned me about my own background with regards to magic. I had to confess that the effects had already appeared in my own life, but in order to defend myself I said that all I wanted to do was to help my fellow man, and that I encouraged people to accept their healing as a gift of

God. The man explained to me, though, that in doing so I was really blaspheming, and treating God as a servant rather than as my Lord. He went on to say that the devil would be behind my work as it is he who seeks to deceive people by this form of blasphemy.

At first I rejected his argument. I could not believe that what he said was true. But his warning remained with me and later I discovered that he had continued to pray for me. And so the battle had begun. My wife joined me in this struggle and finally I was prepared to forsake my magic. But this was easier said than done. I wanted to leave the magic behind me but discovered that by now it held me in its grip. I was a prisoner. We continued to pray and read the Bible together with our children, and in this way sought God's help in our lives. I then had to go into hospital for a serious operation but the strain of the conflict delayed this for just over three weeks until the surgeon thought that I was strong enough to go through with it. The operation was a success and I recovered very quickly and returned to my family. I was filled with joy and thankfulness by this experience.

We were one step nearer to victory. But the battle was not yet over. One day I was reading the passage in Acts 19 where it is written, "And a number of those who practised magic arts brought their books together and burned them in the sight of all." Now I saw what I had to do and so collecting together all the magic books that I had we burned them.

But there was one last area in which we had to gain the victory. My life had become filled with swearing, anger, selfishness, alcohol, smoking, cards, and other unmentionable things, while my wife had been plagued by depressions and similar magical effects. Through the presence of Christ in our lives this last victory was won. My wife was delivered from her depressions, and God worked in my own life freeing me from the habits that had previously held me captive. We had together experienced the truth of Luke 19:10, "The Son of Man came to seek and to save the lost."

The Lord's deliverance had a great effect on my life and I determined that if Christ had helped a great sinner like myself, then he could use me to tell others of the salvation that we can all have in Him. It thus became my aim to reach others who had been bound in the same way as myself, whether consciously or unconsciously. It became obvious to me in my subsequent work to what depths modern man is involved and ensnared by occultism. Yet in spite of this the Word of God remains true: "Where sin increased, grace abounded all the more." The final victory for ever belongs to Jesus Christ our redeemer.

H. Buechler, France

7. Delivered from Darkness

Jochen's life revolved around drinking and girls. He used to drink on average about thirty pints of beer a day. He was seldom sober and if ever he could not get enough to drink, he used to roam around like a wounded animal. He had a temper as well, and at the slightest provocation he would lash out and smash anything within striking distance. On top of this he rejected completely both the idea of God and of the devil. To him it was all nonsense.

One day at the local public house a group was talking about the possibility of making a pact with the devil, and they were exchanging stories of this nature. Many of them laughed off the idea, Jochen being one of them. He went on to say that he was not afraid of meeting the devil, and so when someone challenged him, he agreed to attempt such a meeting for a bet of about £2. Thus one Friday night Jochen found himself at some crossroads outside the village. He drew a circle on the ground and repeated a charm that he had been told would summon Lucifer, and waited for the devil to appear. Nothing happened, and so he returned in triumph to receive his reward.

But his joy was short-lived. That night when he finally went to bed he suddenly saw a horrible face on the wall opposite his bed, and, frozen with fear, he watched as the face slowly advanced until it was less than a foot from his own face. He screamed, and his sister and her husband rushed to his door to see what the matter was. But when they reached the door they found that they could not enter. Something prevented them. The event recurred again and again, and on each occasion the others found it impossible to enter the room. Finally the experience became too much for Jochen and he went to consult his doctor. He was given a thorough examination but the doctor could discover nothing wrong with him. When asked if it could be the result of his drinking the doctor also replied to the negative. Jochen went on to describe in detail the face that had appeared to him, and also the background to the experience. The doctor was thoughtful, and then warned Jochen that if he really wanted to be healed he would have to do a right-about-turn and hand his life over to Christ. Unlike many of his profession, the doctor was a believing Christian and seriously believed in the power of Satan to rule people's lives through fear. Jochen accepted his advice and he began to seek God in earnest. In the end he experienced a complete deliverance not only from the apparitions but also from his addiction to alcohol and women. His life was entirely changed through his contact with the living Christ. Seventeen years have now passed by since that time, and Jochen is now an active worker in his church, having been elected to his own church council. The power of Christ has indeed delivered him from the power of darkness. He is now able to praise

God with the same words as those of the early Christians, "Giving thanks to the Father who has qualified us to share in the inheritance of the saints in light. He has delivered us from the dominion of darkness and transferred us to the kingdom of his beloved Son" (Col. 1:12–13).

8. *And the Devils Left Her*

A friend of mine recounted to me his most difficult counselling experience. It concerned his sister-in-law.

For many years the patient had suffered from depressions, doubts and other difficulties connected with her faith. She took a violent dislike to the Scriptures, to the church and even to pictures on Christian themes. She would be immediately upset if anyone tried to give her any Christian counsel. A psychologist would have said that her condition was due to an over-religious upbringing but the case was exactly the opposite. The mother had been even more violently opposed to the things of God than her daughter. The daughter had all the signs characteristic of a demoniac, and she could at one moment be violently antagonistic to God and at the next moment she might have a desire and a longing to become a Christian. The psychiatrist would call this a split personality. The patient also used to see ghosts in her own bedroom as a child, and when on these occasions she had screamed out in fear, the ghosts had attacked her.

The woman admitted that she had often in her life resorted to fortune-tellers and that her mother had been in the habit of laying cards. Another fact that only came to the surface in the later stages of counselling was that as an unborn child her mother had subscribed her to the devil.

Before she had come to seek the advice of my friend, it turned out that she had already sought the help of a fanatical sect, one of whose members had laid hands on her and prayed for her. The result had only been a worsening of the disturbances, and since that time she had stayed away from everything religious, as she put it. She had subsequently been treated by several neurologists and had even been in a mental hospital for a short time. The diagnosis that the doctors had continually made is significant. Again and again she was told that mentally she was quite healthy, in spite of the fact that she was suffering from some psychic disorder.

When the patient came to my friend for counselling one of his first questions was, "Have you been involved in any sins connected with magic?" On the confession that she had, it was then pointed out to her from the Bible where the road to deliverance lay. The woman at once began to tremble, and she started to swear and to curse terribly. Yet it still appeared that she had a desire to be delivered. My friend noticed that every time he tried praying with her she would begin to twitch and move awkwardly. His impression was that he was dealing with a demonic influence or possession. This thought was augmented by the fact that when he commanded the evil powers in the name of Jesus, the woman quietened down. One day when he had done just this the woman could even find it in herself to believe that Jesus had in fact died for her redemption and forgiveness.

But now a dramatic battle began to take place. It started with the woman attacking her counsellor with a knife the very next day. He had again commanded in the name of Jesus and the woman had again quietened down. She had then gone so far as to apologize for her behaviour. Later that same day on attending a meeting taken by my friend she expressed a desire to take part in the communion service, but as she had attempted to take the bread and wine she had begun to tremble. It was only after her brother-in-law had commanded in the name of Jesus that she had been able to partake of the emblems. Nevertheless she returned home that night strengthened.

The second phase of the battle ended up with her being sent to a mental hospital. Having stayed for a week at her brother-in-law's house she returned home to her own family. But each time she returned to her relatives her condition worsened. It was at this time that Billy Graham held a crusade in Zurich and my friend invited his sister-in-law along to one of the meetings. She went, but during the message she again trembled all over. Her brother-in-law prayed with her and she stopped trembling, but a few days later she had another relapse and attempted to commit suicide. The doctors thought that it was her environment, and had her removed to hospital. But even there she found it impossible to sleep no matter what sedatives were given her. Next she was put into the hands of a psychiatrist and committed to a mental hospital. The treatment of insulin etc. that she received there was also to no avail. My own experience tells me that hers was not a case for the medical world but one for the Christian counsellor. Many forms of mental illness do belong in the hands of a psychiatrist, but a person who is demonically subjected belongs in Christian hands. It is sad to admit that there are too few Christians ready and willing to help in this field.

A short mission was held at the woman's church after this and she was invited to go. However, on hearing one of the messages the patient got up angrily and ran out of the church shouting, "I am going to kill myself, I am going to kill myself." Her brother-in-law ran after her and took her into his house while she was still shouting that something was going to happen that night and that either she or the preacher would have to die. My friend spoke to her and said, "Nobody is going to die because Jesus has been victorious." He prayed with her and she was able to leave the room quietly once more and have a restful night.

In the next phase of the battle a new factor entered the case. The following Sunday without any special invitation the patient took part in all three Sunday services. Afterwards she asked if she could speak with the evangelist and he too had the impression when talking to her that there were demonic powers at work. He asked her, "Have you ever engaged in magic or spiritism or fortune-telling, or anything of this nature?" She again admitted that she had. The evangelist thus began to command the evil powers that were bedevilling the woman to depart. In the meantime her brother-in-law had discovered more about the influence that her mother had had upon her, and being in the same room as his sister-in-law and the evangelist he began to pray that she would be delivered from her mother's sins and subjection. Suddenly she jumped up and attacked the evangelist and a strange voice burst from her lips: "This is my daughter. She must die." Her brother-in-law at once recognized the situation and replied, "Never, she must not die. You must release her from your power." The voice answered, "My daughter belongs to the devil. I subscribed her to the devil as a child." My friend again replied, "You have no right over her life. The blood of Jesus is sufficient for your daughter. She has been bought by the blood of Christ." The strange voice then went on, "If I give up my daughter I will go out of my mind. If I give in I will go mad." (It should be noted that at this time the patient's mother was still alive.) Her brother-in-law answered, "Even if you go out of your mind you must leave your daughter alone and never return and plague her." The patient was by now completely exhausted and she began to pray quietly. Events such as this have often occurred throughout the history of the Church, where strange voices have spoken out of people, and Mark 5 records a similar instance. I have several cases recorded in my own files.

The fifth phase was even more dramatic. The next

evening the visiting evangelist challenged the audience to accept Christ. The woman decided in her own heart to follow Christ and have faith in Him, and for several days she was filled with a feeling of great joy. But then one morning at breakfast she began to tremble. Her face became distorted and in her fear she called out for her brother-in-law. He rushed in and at once started to pray for her. This time it made no difference. She cried out that there was some strange force at work within her. My friend commanded the alien power to leave her. Then a new voice exclaimed, "No, I will not leave her." It was not the same voice that they had heard before. "Who are you?" my friend asked. "I am an old gipsy", came the reply, and at that moment the woman grabbed for a bread knife and tried to attack her brother-in-law. He took hold of her arm and continued to pray. She quietened down and let go of the knife and began to cry. She had been completely conscious the whole time.

And now we come to the climax of the whole affair. The next day this second voice again started to speak out of the patient. "You are scared. You are frightened", it said mockingly. "No, I am not", replied her brother-in-law. An ugly laugh came from the patient. "You cannot do a thing. We are legions and can defend ourselves to the last. Even the doctors did not know who was behind the sickness." For the first time in the conversation my friend's wife burst in, "If you are legions then be driven into the swine." "No, we want to stay in people. We will come into you." Her husband now answered, "That is impossible as we belong to Christ." "Then we will go into your children. We have already made your son ill." (It was true that their son was ill at the time.) "We would have made him worse if we had had permission." Again my friend replied, "You are not allowed to do that. All our children belong to Jesus." "Then we will come into your church and destroy it. We know which people are off guard." "You can't do that either as Christ is guarding our church." Suddenly the patient turned and started running out of the house but her brother-in-law caught hold of her by the arm and pushed her down on to the couch. Again she tried to take hold of a knife. "Come out of her", commanded my friend. "Why won't you stop praying?" said the voices. "We won't stop praying until you have come out of her." "What do you gain through saving one soul?" the voices asked. "One soul is worth more to the Saviour than the whole world." The voices went on, "We will not come out of this woman, because if we do she will go home and witness to others. Stop your praying. There are others praying in the house." My friend had not realized that his children were by now praying for the woman and so he said, "Yes, the Saviour is praying for you." "No, no, He is not praying for us", said the voices excitedly. The woman with that took an angry glance at a picture of Christ that was hanging in the room. "That's true, He is not praying for you spirits, He is praying for you, poor woman." "We can't stand this praying much longer", cried the voices. By now a period of three hours had elapsed since the battle had begun. With his wife praying at his side and his ten children praying in another room the man once more commanded the unclean spirits to depart in the name of Jesus. Suddenly the woman became very quiet and she began to pray and to cry at the same time. She was delivered, but for a whole day she suffered some terrible pains in her body. When the last day of the mission finally arrived she gave her testimony before all those assembled, and from that moment the pains disappeared completely. Next Sunday she took part in communion and whereas previously she had always felt the evil forces trying to strangle her on such occasions she was now able to take part with complete freedom. Christ had won the battle, He had undone her fetters. It was for this purpose that the Son of God was manifest, to destroy the works of the devil.

Otto Vogt, Switzerland

9. Stronger is He that is in You

Near Madang in New Guinea is situated the mission hospital Jagaum. One day a young Papuan Christian called Koimbo was brought into the hospital. He had been the first person to carry the message of the gospel from the coastlands to his own tribe in the mountains. His tribe had been idol worshippers but few of them had been prepared to forsake their evil spirits and believe in the name of Christ. The small group of Christians was of course bitterly persecuted by their fellow tribesmen. Koimbo's own life had often been threatened, yet his enemies now feared to kill him as openly as they would have done ten years ago. They therefore called in the help of a notorious witch-doctor in order to get rid of him. This man accepted the money offered him and set about his devilish work. He called upon the spirits to punish Koimbo because as a Christian he was interfering with and threatening their own powers.

Koimbo used to hold meetings for the Christians in the jungle. To hold them in the villages would have been impossible as the villagers would have prevented this. Nevertheless even these meetings did not pass unobserved, and it was at one of these meetings that the witch-doctor attacked. Koimbo was reading the Scriptures aloud when all at once he exclaimed, "I can't see anything." His friends jumped to his aid, and took him aside hoping that he would regain his sight. But they waited in vain. The other villagers were delighted.

For a few weeks Koimbo remained in his hut both physically and spiritually weakened. It was then that his friends brought him to Jagaum. As they were leading him out of the village all the villagers together with the old witch-doctor came out of their huts and mocked and derided him. "Now you can see that our spirits are stronger than the Christians' God", they cried.

Koimbo was warmly received at the hospital, but after a thorough examination the doctor said that his eyes had been completely blinded and that there was no hope of him ever regaining his sight. This was very hard for him to accept, and he was near to despair.

That evening the nurse came to his bedside. "How are you?" she asked. Koimbo reached out for her hand. "O sister, it is not my blindness that I am worried about, but it is that I can no longer feel God's presence with me and I can only believe that I have been given over into the hands of the evil spirits, and this is the worst thing." These words cut right into the nurse's heart. This was wrong. Satan has no right to be victorious.

"Koimbo, let us pray together to our Lord. He will surely hear us. The evil spirits cannot have the last word. Jesus has overcome them." With that the two of them began to pray. They continued all night reminding God of His promises, and remembering His power to give sight to the blind and to deliver those oppressed by the devil.

Suddenly as the new day was just dawning, Koimbo let out a shout. "Sister, I can see you. I can see you. Anuto (God) has healed me. Anuto is great." The other nurses and attendants gathered around, and a deep sense of joy and gratitude descended upon them all.

Koimbo now wanted to return to his village. He wanted to be a living witness to his fellow villagers that Jesus Christ is stronger than the prince of this world.

10. If the Son shall Make You Free . . .

One day a messenger arrived at our mission station in Lishui. He asked if some of the Christian women would go with him to the house of one of the native Christians. A few of us set out and came to the house where we found a native woman in a terribly emaciated state. It turned out that she had been carried there in order to get help from the Christians' God. The journey had taken them over six hours and she was introduced to us as the sister-in-law of the family.

As was often the case we discovered that the woman had been plagued by a spirit called Fan yiao, who caused a lot of trouble among the tribes. The woman had sought the help of many idols but all to no avail. Now she asked the God of the Christians to show his power. As she told her story some of the Christians were frightened because this particular spirit Fan yiao had afflicted the natives in a terrible way.

Anyway, when the woman had finished we began to sing the song 'The Great Physician is now near'. This song is much loved among the Christians as the name of Jesus is often mentioned in it and they know that the devil flees when he hears that name. We then went on to tell the woman the message of Jesus. In spite of the fact that she did not understand much of what we said, she did at least grasp the fact that Jesus could help her. It was to this truth that she clung. We prayed for her, and went on to teach her how to call on the name of Jesus and how to trust Him. We returned again the next day and rejoiced to find that she had passed the night in peace. We thus arranged that two of the Christian women should visit her each day to pray with her and encourage her, and we now found that the woman was no longer plagued at night as she had been in the past.

But this did not last, for some time later her two visitors were greeted with cries of, "He found me again, he found me again." And true enough the spirit or demon had attacked her that night in the form of a black cat. One of the Christians at once asked her, "Have you had anything to do with idols again?" At first the woman refused to answer, but finally she admitted that her husband had visited her and had wanted to sacrifice a pig, because as he said, "You can't be too sure that it was the Christian God who healed you." The woman had agreed. Her husband had then left with the intention of making the sacrifice. It was that very night that Fan yiao had struck again. The Christians at once advised her to send a message to her husband forbidding him to go through with the offering. They pointed out that the honour belonged solely to Jesus Christ. She sent the message.

Following this experience the woman begged them to let her be taken into the mission station. And so it was that she moved in to sleep with one of the Christian women at the station. She stayed there for three weeks and every day was able to hear the Word of God. Wanting to return to her home in November, and feeling confident because of her continued freedom from attacks, the woman decided to leave the mission. She said that she would return at Christmas to spend that time with them if she was still well. And so the time passed and the day of her expected return arrived. But there was no sign of the woman. One of the Christians offered to go the next day on the long journey to see the woman. But it was not necessary for on that very day she arrived full of joy at the mission station. She had been free from the attacks ever since leaving them and it was only the floods that had prevented her coming sooner. The woman was full of praise and thanksgiving for her deliverance and our fears were unfounded. She was the only Christian in a very large area but over the following years she continued to be faithful to her Lord. Finally we lost contact with her however, as the area became the centre of unrest due to the Russo-Japanese war.

11. In My Name They shall Cast out Demons

In one of our outstations we had a faithful Chinese evangelist who had a lot of authority in prayer. Around the mission station there were quite a number of cases of possession and it was amazing how quick the Chinese were at recognizing the difference between a person who was possessed and one who was mentally ill. In this they were better than many a European psychiatrist. If our particular evangelist thought that someone was possessed he would call a prayer group together and sometimes they would fast and pray for days until the person was delivered from the evil spirits. Once they had prayed and fasted every evening for over seven weeks until one particular woman was delivered. The following story indicates how hard the battle can be for a person's soul.

Close to the mission station there lived a family in which for many generations at least one of the members had been possessed by the demon named Fan yiao. If the possessed person died then Fan yiao passed on into another member of the family. The father had been possessed but he had died in agony and the spirit had passed over into an aunt. She was not expected to live very long and the remaining mother and daughter feared the day when they too would be possessed by the same spirit. At that time another missionary and myself were able to bring the gospel to this area. The mother and daughter came within sound of the gospel but although they responded to it they did not make a full committal to Christ. Then the aunt died. The daughter went to the funeral which was conducted by a pagan priest. During the ceremony she was taken possession of by the spirit Fan yiao. The frightened mother brought her to the church hall begging the Christians there to help her. They began praying for the girl and that evening she was delivered.

Some time later the girl married. Her husband was not a Christian, but she had to marry him as they had been betrothed for many years. After the wedding her parents-in-law forbade her to continue attending the Christian meetings. They took her Bible away and burned it. But immediately after that Fan yiao took control of her. Strange voices used to speak out of her and she was unable to do any work. Her parents-in-law were very frightened and they now asked the evangelist to come and pray for the girl. He again prayed for her and the result was that she was again delivered. She was overjoyed, but the parents-in-law, who had promised to buy her a new Bible and to let her meet with the Christians, now changed their minds and stopped her from going to the service the next Sunday. But the same thing happened. Fan yiao took control again. This time the heathen couple realized that they had to take Jesus seriously. They arrived at the mission station carrying the girl on a special chair. The same group of people began to pray for her again. But now it was not so easy. For three consecutive evenings they met to pray and to fast, but Fan yiao would not yield. Then the evangelist decided that it was time to act. He approached the possessed girl and said , "Your time is up. You must now leave her. I charge you in the name of Jesus." Suddenly a man's voice burst out of the girl's mouth. "This praying is unbearable. Who can stand it?" Again the girl was liberated. The parents-in-law now kept their promise and the girl was allowed to practise her faith. Fan yiao never returned. She was completely healed.

These two examples show us that man is not only

subject to mental and emotional illnesses but also to demonic influences that transcend all geographical and racial boundaries. Similar cases to these can be observed all over the world, and the picture drawn by the New Testament is the same. Because possession is a biblical fact, an unbelieving psychiatrist or doctor will be unable to deal with it. If a person can only think in terms of three dimensions then he will never understand things relating to the divine and the demonic. But above the phenomenon of possession stands the glorious victory which Christ has had over all the powers of darkness. A person who has given his allegiance to Jesus Christ partakes in the same victory. It was Jesus himself who said, "In my name they shall cast out demons" (Mark. 16:17).

12. The Victory Belongs to the Lord

A missionary was engaged in work in New Guinea. The area in which she worked was much infected by magic and many of the natives lived under the ban of the witch-doctors. The missionary had made little progress there and during her times of prayer she had often felt approached by a terribly evil force. She informed her friends at home of this and asked them to stand by her in prayer that the devil would lose his hold on the mission field where she was. In addition to the evil powers around her she had often been threatened by the presence of wild animals. Every time she had attempted to visit a certain village where a notorious witch-doctor lived she had been prevented from doing so, because she had met snakes on the way there. At first she had thought that this was only a coincidence but later she found it to be otherwise. One day the missionary actually managed to visit the village. Unsuspectingly she entered one particular hut in order to give the occupant a tract. As she spoke to the woman in the hut a terrible feeling came over her has if someone behind her was just about to kill her. She turned round and saw a man in a corner whom she had not noticed before. As his eyes caught hers she felt as though she was coming under his spell. She tried to pray but because of the man's eyes she could not. Finally all that she could do was to challenge the man in the name of Jesus. The result was astonishing. The man fell to the ground and began to whimper and to moan on the floor. There is something similar in this story to the occasion when the Philistine god Dagon fell to the ground when confronted with the ark of the Lord.

It was only later that the missionary discovered that the man in the hut was the village's chief witch-doctor, and that the natives recognized his ability to control and to use wild animals for his own evil purposes.

13. There is Power in the Blood of the Lamb

We had arranged to conduct a week's mission, holding the meetings in the local school. All was going well, or so I thought, as I stood up to speak at the first meeting. However, as I proceeded it became more and more difficult for me to go on speaking as it felt as though someone was trying to hold my mouth shut. Walking home that night I was covered with perspiration. I had never experienced this before. I was only a young evangelist, but I knew that there was a resistance to the message that was completely foreign to me. Could I use the messages that I had already prepared? Did the people need something different? With these thoughts going through my mind, I climbed into bed.

What was that? I had just switched off the light when I saw a large shadowy object in front of me. Then a voice said quite clearly, "If you dare to continue with this mission then I will kill you. These people belong to me." What could I say? I realized that there was only one answer. "If the Lord has commissioned me then no one can stand in the way." The voice replied, "All right, I will kill you." At that moment I was seized by a feeling of cramp in my arms and legs, which soon spread all over my body and finally concentrated on the area of my heart. I could not move and I became quite cold. I lay there for about two hours until at last the pains left me. Now I knew for certain that this enemy wanted to kill me. Yet at the same time I was assured that he would only be able to do this if the Lord permitted it.

The days that followed were very difficult ones for me, but I soon discovered where the source of the trouble lay. Many of the villagers practised either fortune-telling or magic and some of them were also plagued by these same evil powers. I found it almost impossible to prepare new messages for the meetings. I tried to pray but all I could do was to kneel and sigh. The same cramp-like pains attacked me each night although I never saw the apparition again. I did not know what to do. I was convinced that God had called me to the village to hold the mission or else I would have soon given it up.

The men in the church could give me no advice and they did not even seem to take the matter seriously. Finally I was led to visit a dear old servant of God. I told him of my experience and how that I was completely at a loss as to what to do. When people had come to me for counsel I had been unable to give them any advice at all.

It was the Lord himself who had led me to this man. He told me of things about which I should have known before I left Bible school although possibly I would not have understood them at the time. Yet in a way he told me nothing new. I knew already that there was power available to us through Christ's blood, and yet I had never known it in experience. Not only did my own attacks cease when I placed myself under the protection of the blood of Christ but I also saw God's power begin to work in the lives of others in the village. We were able to overcome through the blood of the Lamb.

The reason the Son of God appeared was to destroy the works of the devil (1 John 3:8).

Otto Haeni, an evangelist, Switzerland

14. Deprived of Power

It was early in 1959 when we received a telephone call from a dentist. He inquired about our telephone ministry, how we ran it and its aim and object. On answering his questions he stated that he would come round and visit us personally and so we made an appointment. When the dentist did in fact come, he showed marked signs of nervousness. We noticed though, that he tried to catch our eyes in a fixed stare and we felt an evil atmosphere about us, for it seemed as though he was trying to put us under his spell. Since my partner and I both had the same feeling we went outside for a moment and prayed. When we returned we carried on a disjointed conversation but the stranger left after about half an hour. As he left we felt almost contaminated by his evil influence and so we prayed earnestly for cleansing.

The next morning the dentist rang us up again and asked us if we had felt anything the previous night. We asked him what we were supposed to have felt but he hung up at once. The same happened again the following morning, and when he hung up a second time we were extremely puzzled by his behaviour.

A few days went by and then he called us again. He asked us to pray for him and confessed that the devil had given him specific instructions to fight our telephone ministry. He was very distressed but he went on to tell us that as a student he had subscribed himself to the devil with his own blood. He said that there was no turning back although he wanted to follow our advice. A few days later he called again. In desperation he told us that he had tried to kill us but his method had failed. It had bounced back on himself. A far stronger force had been present in us than the one which he possessed. He could not accept the Word of God as he belonged to Satan, and Satan was driving him to his own death.

The next day a post card arrived. There was a cross in the top right hand corner and underneath it was written, "When you receive this letter I will be dead." Soon afterwards the police called and told us that the dentist had shot himself. They had found his body with a book on magic lying beside him entitled 'The Mirror of Solomon'.

This unfortunate man had plagued people for many years. Yet his contract with the devil had led to his own destruction. Here we have illustrated the fact that the power of Jesus Christ far exceeds the power of Satan. And does it not prove too, that a Christian's prayer is never in vain? Jesus has conquered both hell and the devil. Stronger is He that is in us than he that is in the world. He has deprived the devil of his power. "He disarmed the principalities and powers and made a public example of them, triumphing over them in the cross" (Col. 2:15).

Werner Ambuehl, an evangelist, Switzerland

15. At the Name of Jesus every Knee shall Bow

Shortly after the Second World War when I had escaped from the hands of the Russians I found myself suffering from depressions as a result of malnutrition. These emotional disturbances increased and so I sought the help of doctors. One doctor prescribed opium drops to quieten me down, but this did not help. Another doctor took me off medicine and tried psychotherapy. This too was not really effective as it only proved beneficial when I was actually in the presence of the doctor in question.

It was then that I reverted to my old profession, that of a Protestant minister. Yet as my work increased, my illness worsened. My wife again called for the doctor and it was then that the Lord intervened. An evangelist happened to visit us at that time but I tried to avoid him as I did not really want to talk to him or to anyone.

My wife however, talked with him, and he told her that he thought he should pray for me and lay hands on me. I refused. This was a completely new idea to me although I was a minister. I had never heard of anything like this before, not even when I was training for the ministry, and so I turned down his suggestion.

Yet my wife persisted in encouraging me and finally won. The evangelist thus laid his hands on me and prayed for me. Yet nothing happened. Next day he returned. When he discovered that there had been no improvement he asked if I had ever been oppressed by or subjected to anything in my life. This made me very indignant. I was a Protestant minister. What could oppress me?

The brother went on to describe to me the various sins associated with magic and witchcraft, and he pointed out that the area in which I lived was infested with such practices. He went on to describe how the sins of one's parents could be passed on to oneself. Slowly the truth dawned on me. As a child my father had been sick. Medical help had proved useless and so his mother had sought the help of magic charming. The magic treatment had been an immediate success.

The evangelist reminded me of the commandment that says that the sins of the fathers shall be visited on the children to the third and fourth generation. Did I recognize my father's action to be sin? Yes, I did. We knelt down and I confessed this together with my own sins.

It was a repentance to life. Through faith I was able to be forgiven, and I committed my life to the Lord Jesus.

The evangelist laid hands on me again and prayed for me. A wonderful sense of peace came over me and I later felt as if I was walking on air. This sense of joy and peace continued with me for weeks. For the first time in my life I appreciated the words of Paul in Phil. 3, "Our commonwealth is in heaven." My whole life, everything I did was transfigured by the love of Christ. The Bible, my work and my ministry took on a completely different appearance.

When I later visited my doctor he examined me and then said that the results were amazing. I was a different man both physically and mentally. My depressions never returned. This miracle took place after I had been a minister for several years, and it was a lowly evangelist who had been the tool that God had used to heal me.

The miracle that God had worked in my life affected the whole church. My preaching was renewed and the congregation noticed this. My main aim was now to uplift the name of Jesus, and the word did not return again void. People were converted and in the surrounding districts small revivals began to break out. It had previously been impossible to hold mid-week meetings but now prayer meetings and Bible studies sprang up instantaneously. God had lit a fire and continued to keep the flame burning.

The very name of Jesus became the centre of my ministry. His name now meant power to me, it was the power of God unto salvation. It is now my burning desire to tell others of all that this name contains. "There is salvation in no one else, for there is no other name under heaven given among men by which we must be saved."

Rev. Berthold Schoof, Germany

16. *Jesus, our Living Lord and Saviour*

I first became interested in spiritualism when my family moved to Woking in Surrey just before the Second World War. Some friends of ours invited us along to the local spiritualistic church and soon we were regularly attending their meetings. At one of these meetings my mother was told by a clairvoyant that she had psychic powers and was a medium. And so as time went on we became more involved, and soon we were holding regular séances in our own house. I would often help my parents set out the chairs in preparation for the meetings in the evening, and I was often present when my mother, acting as the medium, went into a trance before contact with the spirits was made. Once at a séance we saw my mother's head and shoulders gradually transfigured into that of an old wizened Chinaman with a long beard who was supposed to be her spirit guide named Chang. There was another occasion when we saw some ectoplasm streaming out of my mother, and still other times when the large oak table around which we were sitting and which normally required two men to lift, would of itself rise slowly off the floor till it was hovering about a foot in the air. Once when I had just returned home on leave from Norway my mother was asked by some visitors to hold a séance. She consented and when she went into a trance she began speaking in a foreign language. It was Norwegian, and normally speaking she did not know a word of this language. It was left to me to translate the message to those present. She had also on other occasions spoken in German, Chinese and some other language that sounded like Arabic.

But there is another side to the story. After each séance my mother was completely exhausted. Also as time went on she began to suffer from depressions and had fits of temper in which she would scream and shout and even froth at the mouth. On one such occasion she came at me with a knife and it was only my army training that prevented me from being seriously injured. Her memory too was affected and she became mentally unbalanced. In my own life after I had come into contact with spiritualism the tendency was for me to become enslaved to smoking and drinking, and the violent streak in my nature now often came to the surface.

It was at this time that God stepped into our lives. My mother met a Christian in the Salvation Army and as soon as he discovered that she was an active spiritualist he spoke with her about the dangers of spiritualism and began to invite both my mother and my stepfather along to the Salvation Army services and meetings. Meanwhile I was away in the forces but God had His hand on me too. The padre of our battalion got talking with me one day and invited me to his house for a meal. He soon discovered my background for I readily admitted that I was a spiritualist and that for me spiritualism was the only true religion. He tried to show me from the Scriptures that this was not the case, but I was very antagonistic and once I even got up from the table in the middle of a meal and walked out of his house. Nevertheless it gradually dawned on me that he was right and although I did not become a Christian at that time I at least became sympathetic towards the Christian message.

Then in 1947 my mother became a Christian and within a couple of weeks my stepfather also accepted Christ as his Saviour. My mother told me later that at first, after she had committed her life to Christ, the depressions and other psychic troubles that had plagued her seemed to come almost every day as if the devil was throwing everything he had at her. In order to overcome the temptation to slip back into her old ways she found it necessary to pray earnestly sometimes for hours on end. There were times when she had to call in a Christian neighbour so that they could together pray for her deliverance. And God did deliver her. It was an experience similar to the withdrawal period which drug addicts have to go through if they hope to be delivered from their addiction.

My own conversion took place in 1952 at a tent mission in Woking after I had finally left the forces and come home again. At one of the meetings I asked the Lord Jesus to come into my life, and this He did. It was a revolution and my life was completely changed by the presence of Christ within me. By this time both my parents had grown considerably in the Christian faith and they were actually taking an active part in this particular tent mission helping the evangelist by singing and playing the organ at the meetings.

Although over the years my mother's memory carried the scar of the wound it had suffered when she had been actively involved in spiritism and although Satan still attempted to rob her of her peace of mind, she was able to overcome through the power of prayer. In fact in the last year of her life she seemed to be so full of the Lord that all signs of her previous troubles disappeared, and when she finally died in 1964, she died with the word 'Hallelujah' upon her lips.

I can thus praise God that He has not only kept me by His grace but that He also kept my mother and continues to keep my stepfather in the knowledge that Jesus Christ is our Saviour. I can truly say that today I know that there is a devil for I have seen him at work in this world. But God has taught me the difference between Christ and Satan, and I rejoice to know that Jesus has proved Himself to be my living Lord and Saviour.

Alan Watkins, England